G000167846

BEYOND THE

WHERE FAITH AND BUSINESS MEET

BOTTOM LINE

BEYOND THE

WHERE FAITH AND BUSINESS MEET

BOTTOM LINE

WILLIAM LAWRENCE

WITH JACK TURPIN

PRAXIS
BOOKS

MOODY PRESS

CHICAGO

© 1994 by
WILLIAM D. LAWRENCE

All rights reserved. No part of this book may be reproduced in any form without permission in writing from the publisher, except in the case of brief quotations embodied in critical articles or reviews.

All Scripture quotations, unless indicated, are taken from the *Holy Bible, New International Version.*® NIV.® Copyright © 1973, 1978, 1984 International Bible Society. Used by permission of Zondervan Publishing House. All rights reserved.

Scripture quotations marked NASB are from the *New American Standard Bible,* © 1960, 1962, 1963, 1968, 1971, 1972, 1973, 1975, and 1977 by The Lockman Foundation, and are used by permission.

The term "praxis" originates from Greek philosophy. It refers to almost any kind of activity a person is likely to perform, in particular, all kinds of business and political activity. It also relates to moral conduct, practical application of knowledge, utilizing common sense, following an established practice, applying an established truth, doing what is right.

ISBN 0-8024-1082-0

1 3 5 7 9 10 8 6 4 2

Printed in the United States of America

To those quiet heroes I have known
who everyday go below the bottom line
and by faith do business
with virtue, dignity, and honor

CONTENTS

WHERE FAITH AND BUSINESS MEET

What lies beyond the bottom line, where faith and business meet?

Beyond the bottom line is

The core of the conscience
where life's decisions are made and character is forged

The heart of the soul
where right and wrong meet in tension and stress

The inner sanctum of the spirit
where life's battles are fought:
the battle of integrity versus expediency
the battle of truth versus deception
the battle of contentment versus greed
the battle of purity versus pleasure

The foundation of life,
the secret closet where we go alone with God
to establish our values, make our commitments,
build our beliefs,
and from which we return to live out our convictions

Beyond the bottom line is
the place of trust,
where the ultimate choice is made:
self or God

INTRODUCTION

No one who reads the business pages or *Fortune* or watches the news can deny the fact that corporate America is facing a crisis of character. Looking out for Number 1 seems to be the dominant drive of directors, presidents, investors, managers, brokers, reporters, virtually all fields in the business world.

There are many explanations, but relatively few reasons. Greed has become honorable, even admirable among some, in these days; absolutes have been replaced by relativism, conscience by excuses, character by conniving. Insider trading, secret foreign bank accounts, savings and loans rip-offs—the dirty laundry list is long and growing longer.

Money and ambition seem to be the driving forces that stir our times and direct our destiny. The idea of public virtue has been replaced by special interests, then by personal interests, resulting in a destructive individualism so that "today, America no longer leads the world and is itself leaderless."[1]

A nation without an ethical norm cannot long maintain its own strength or stand in support of others. Thus, ethics is one of the central issues of our day, an issue which we must pursue with disciplined, almost desperate, diligence.

If there is any one segment of our society that should meet and model ethical excellence, Christians are that segment. Christians in business must become a new breed of heroes, a quiet kind of hero committed to character as their top profit and spiritual influence as their greatest contribution. Such people may never be famous or influential, but their mass impact can bring a brilliant light to bear on the darkness of our society.

But how do Christians in business become such quiet heroes? What will be their distinctive mark? It must be integrity. Certainly integrity is an essential ingredient for ethics, the most desired characteristic followers want in their business leaders. In a survey taken of about 1,500 managers from around the United States, the most frequent responses in order of occurrence were integrity, competence, and leadership. Clearly, "honesty is absolutely essential to leadership."[2]

Yet there is a question about integrity. In an age of relativism, who can define it with authority? In this time of drifting values, integrity can mean whatever its possessor professes it to be. Integrity is a lot like the U.S. dollar, a paper standard, worth only the value the government gives it. To establish a true ethic for the business world we need a gold standard, a double eagle: we need a clearly defined standard of right and wrong. For the Christian in business, absolutes form the basis of the true ethic, the gold standard backed by the character and Word of God. God's truth defines and determines what is and what is not ethical.

Here is the undergirding principle supporting this book: the greatest profit in business is the profit of pleasing God by being what He wants, doing what He says, and showing what He is like. Men and women who do this become the new heroes of our time, the quiet heroes who help clean up the foul, polluted river of business ethics and restore it to a refreshing beauty in which the predator fish are held back by the dam of right and wrong. These quiet heroes themselves will form that dam by leading corporations, managing people, negotiating deals, making money, meeting human needs, ministering in churches, and serving their families in ways that please the holy God.

The aim of this book is to help its readers become such heroes. Each chapter concludes with a section entitled "Beyond the Bottom Line," which shows how to apply the principles of the chapter and encourages readers to do so.

During the past twenty-five years, as a pastor (twelve years) and a seminary professor (thirteen years), one of my greatest delights has been to spend time with those in the business world who are serving Christ in a strategic ministry in the area of commerce. Out of these years of fellowship has come a burden for a book on business ethics from a Christian perspective written for those who seek to please Christ in their life pursuits.

The problem, of course, is that I am only half qualified to write such a book. I know the biblical principles that should govern a Christian business ethic, but I have not lived in the business atmosphere. It is my providential fortune, however, to have friends who have spent their entire working lives in the competitive dollars-and-cents setting of the business world. A number of them, from lawyers and developers to corporate executives, entrepreneurs, and bankers, have made themselves available to interact with the principles I have developed and to add the crucial quality of reality to my thinking. We have worked together to discuss and apply these principles, to develop case studies, and to combine our strengths to produce what we believe will be a helpful guide through the minefield of ethical Christian living in today's business setting.

I have received great assistance in the writing of this book from Jack Turpin. Founder of Hamilton Hall Mark, member of the Texas Sports Hall of Fame, chairman of the board at Dallas Theological Seminary, husband, father of three, and grandfather of twelve, Jack is a man who has attempted to implement his faith at every level of his personal life and his business career. To help the readers of this book, he has given me his own story as well as his insights into the business mind, both of which have helped me immeasurably.

One other person should be mentioned as a singular contributor to this effort, and that is my wife, Lynna. She has served as my first editor who has worked to make sense out of what I've been trying to say before it all goes to the publisher. Without Lynna's help and patience, I would never have made it. She has labored over these pages in order to make it possible for me to communicate this message, and I am grateful for her help.

Finally, I am grateful for the encouragement and support of my longtime friend Don H. Johnson, president of the structural steel division and Stearns Airport Equipment Company of Trinity Industries, whose interest and influence has made this book possible.

Our prayers are for you, our readers. Our dream is that you will use these principles to live God's way and leave earth ready to receive heaven's reward rather than to file bankruptcy because you bore no eternal fruit. When you conduct your business ethically, both your life and your death will be a gain on heaven's books.

CHAPTER ONE

THE EXIT OF ETHICS

n the 1990s, ethics appears to be missing in action, taken prisoner-of-war by greed, ambition, and selfish individualism. Some of the most famous names in America now make up its roll call of shame. In recent years, leaders in virtually every area of American life have gone to jail for ethical failure. Businessmen Dennis Levine and Charles Keating, religious leader Jim Bakker, and one-time baseball Hall of Fame shoo-in Pete Rose lead the lineup of those removed from places of leadership, sentenced to prison, or publicly rebuked because of their unethical behavior. Other leaders, not caught, continue to operate without concern for whether their behavior is right and just.

How do we explain the exit of ethics that marks our times? Before we answer that crucial question, some may question whether ethics has actually fled America.

Here's more hard evidence. The authors of *The Day America Told the Truth* declare: "At this time, America has no moral leadership. Americans believe, across the board, that our current political, religious, and business leaders have failed us."[1] According to Patterson and Kim, many Americans

also are convinced that one significant cause of our current business decline is low ethics among executives, another evidence of the loss of moral
leadership.[2]

Retired General H. Norman Schwarzkopf, who led the successful Persian Gulf War after Iraq invaded Kuwait, explained the commonly recognized leadership failure in modern American society by saying, "It's never
a competence problem. It's an ethical and moral crisis. It's a problem of
character."[3]

A FLICKERING CANDLE

American society once adhered to an absolute standard of right-and-
wrong, a standard of light and direction offering guidance through the ethical darkness that so easily envelops modern life. Tragically, this once
powerful beam of light, this absolute standard of right, has been reduced
to a barely flickering candle in many quarters.

Not everyone has turned from ethics, of course. Thousands of companies and millions of people do business ethically, as did their parents
and grandparents before them. They treat customers with respect and
honesty, and they operate with integrity. Yet, there can be no doubt that
we have seen an ethical lapse in the past decade that is unparalleled in
history. The reality of the matter is this: more people today are more willing to do business less ethically than ever before.

American youth share the cynicism of the rest of society, influenced
as they are by the visibility of ethical failure that marks their growing up
period. Michael Josephson of the Josephson Institute for Ethics, has reported his findings on ethical behavior in testimony before the U.S. Congress and state legislatures, and he has appeared on network television to
describe the decline of ethics in America. In his 1990 study of ethical attitudes of high school and college students, he concluded:

> Starting with Watergate, the quantity and intensity of publicized
> instances of misconduct by major institutions and powerful individuals
> was bound to negate any positive ethical messages. . . . Thus, the bad
> habits and attitudes of so many young adults reflect deteriorating ethics
> in society in general exemplified by fallen heroes and a system where it's
> the bottom line that counts. In this system ethics is for wimps, honesty is
> not always the best policy, and cheaters often prosper.[4]

Clearly there has been an exit of ethics in America. The question is
why. What has caused ethical standards to decline in a country that many

other nations look to for moral leadership in democracy and standard of living?

One cause is the acceptance of relativism, the belief that no absolute standards exist. Paul Johnson calls relativism the ethical and moral distortion of Einstein's theory of relativity.[5] Other factors contributing to our moral and ethical decline are the sexual revolution, family disintegration, and leadership hypocrisy.

The health of our nation demands a moral antidote that will revive our sense of right and wrong and restore our society to its once high level of ethical leadership. The Judeo-Christian tradition provides that moral antidote as Margaret Thatcher declared in a speech given before the Church of Scotland. Unless Judeo-Christian values rest at the root of society, society cannot exist, according to Mrs. Thatcher, the former Prime Minister of England. [6] Charles Colson, once involved in the Watergate scandal who subsequently became a Christian and a leader in the prison reform movement, says succinctly, "A society cannot survive without a moral consensus."[7] Colson further asserts, "The reason we have the most terrible crime problem in the world in America today is simple: We've lost our moral consensus. We're people living for ourselves."[8]

John H. McArthur, dean of the Harvard Business School, knows well the need for a moral antidote in our nation. He has "even gone so far as to suggest that his Harvard Business School class of 1959 build a religious chapel on the campus to promote the spiritual values he would like to permeate the school."[9] At their commencement exercises, McArthur "personally pleaded with students not 'to go through life focused only on No. 1.'"[10] Our nation truly is in need of a moral antidote.

Money and ambition are major forces that drive our times. In the time of the greatest economic growth in history we seem to have sunk to the lowest ethical level in our national experience. How did all this come about?

SEARCHING FOR A CURE

Although the headlines make it appear as if this has occurred with lightning speed, such is not the case. This change has not come about rapidly or suddenly, but slowly, incrementally. Commenting on the general nature of change in our society, pollster George Barna has said it is more evolutionary than revolutionary, a series of small shifts in fundamental aspects of life, a kind of ripple effect that has a powerful impact upon our times.

The cumulative effect of these minor alterations has resulted in changes in our world that in reality are far greater than the single, big bang that we have been so steadfastly awaiting. What is happening is more like a Chinese water torture, with the water slowly eroding, one drip at a time, the foundations of our Christian culture.[11]

Robert Bellah, in his insightful work, *Habits of the Heart*, shows the impact of change upon our society by taking us from the roots of our tradition to its present fruit. To do this, he looks at the models that have personified the American ideal from colonial times until today. Bellah tells us that we started as a nation with a biblical model of leadership early in the colonial period, but we had turned from those roots by the beginning of the nineteenth century. Throughout history our model shifted to the independent citizen, then to the entrepreneur, next to the manager and, now, to the new high priest of our time, the therapist.[12] Our society, he says, is sick and in search of a cure, and, since healing is the task of the therapist, the role of healer and the longing for health now typify the ideal in America. A profound sickness marks Western society, a sickness that causes us to cast ethics aside in a selfish search for self-centered health and wholeness.

Of course, nowhere is this sickness more apparent than in corporate America and the financial community. In *Other People's Money*, a book tracing the roots of the savings and loan scandal of the late 1980s, the authors show how the loss of ethics shook our confidence in the honorable pursuit of business. Perhaps no segment in society reveals the condition of our country more completely. Kenneth R. Andrews, former editor of the *Harvard Business Review*, argues that business practices merely reflect the underlying moral character of its employees, nurtured in such American institutions as school and family. In *Ethics in Practice*, Andrews writes,

Any decline in ethical behavior is chargeable to all the institutions of society that deliver morally weak people to the companies they join. Long before people go to work to make a living, family, church, and school have shaped their moral characters. If so, then the corporation may have to eliminate all unethical persons, or more practicably, look to see what it can do to foster moral development and eliminate corporate practices that bring more pressure than is necessary upon a person's ability to resist temptation.[13]

Here is a major clue to the problem. The breakdown is a product of the home, school, church, and work, which means the personal, moral, ethical, and spiritual structures of our society have become so polluted they are less capable of producing healthy and whole people.

ECOLOGY FOR A WHOLE PEOPLE

This cultural support structure can be likened to a kind of ecological system designed to produce the fruit of whole people. When this ecological system is pure, it produces healthy people who know what they believe and who are able to live according to their convictions. This system consists of five elements: the family, the church, the school, government, and relationship networks such as the extended family and friendships developed throughout life.

FLAYING THE FAMILY

In our society, this ecological system has become flawed and faulted. We all recognize the flaying of the family and the destruction this has brought upon us. In her book *Second Chances*, Judith Wallerstein, who has done the most definitive research on family break-up and its fruit, traced the consequences of divorce in some sixty marriages. Hers is the only controlled study showing the effects of a marriage break-up fifteen years after the divorce decree. The children of divorce in particular suffer what may be lifetime scars because they carry within themselves "a cocoon of memories—memories of broken hearts, angry conflicts, ugliness, and sometimes violence; memories of wretchedness, abandonment, and betrayal; memories that are sometimes real, sometimes imagined."[14]

Wallerstein and her colleague Sandra Blakeslee expressed shock several times at the unanticipated destructive results they discovered. The adult children of divorce brought broken hearts to work every day, seeking to exorcise these demon memories, at times willing to do anything to find the personal and emotional freedom that would release them to be themselves and do their best. The authors concluded that a number of the adult children of divorce cannot love freely, and I am convinced this must affect their ability to make ethical decisions.

> Fifteen years after their parents divorced, close to 40 percent of the young adults whom we interviewed have been in therapy at various times to work through issues concerning relationships. Generally, men seek therapy less often than women, but the male and female children of divorce in this study have gone for help in equal numbers.[15]

Other negative elements in family life have contributed to the poisoning of much of this generation. In 1990 *Time* magazine reported:

Every eight seconds of the school day, a child drops out. Every 26 seconds, a child runs away from home. Every 47 seconds, a child is abused or neglected. Every 67 seconds, a teenager has a baby. Every seven minutes, a child is arrested for a drug offense. Every 36 minutes, a child is killed or injured by a gun. Every day 135,000 children bring their guns to school.[16]

Sexual, physical, and verbal abuse, the isolation of children due to the driving materialism of their parents, the emotional alienation in so many homes—all have contributed to a generation with fewer settled standards and healthy parental models than before.

Even children from the most affluent circumstances are at risk. An exchange between Pete Rose and his daughter carried in *USA Today* shows how painful and confusing this situation can be. Pete Rose's daughter told reporters, "I don't know why he never spent any time with us. All we wanted him to do was to spend time with us. He never liked us." When the reporters told this to him, he said, "I don't know what she's complaining about. I just bought her a Mercedes last week!" Few statements capture the condition of the family and its breakdown more succinctly than this: a daughter in pain and a father attempting to relieve her pain with a Mercedes rather than a relationship.

When we look at divorce, "we gaze at no less than our most fundamental values—the values by which we measure the meaning and worth of human relationships, of love, of the family itself. And profound changes in the family can only mean profound changes in society as a whole."[17] Divorce brings "a weakening of our unspoken moral commitments to our children,"[18] which means that growing up in America is radically different from what it was a generation ago when families were stable and large numbers of children had a sense of security through their homes. Since the 1970s divorce has been on an upward spiral. The result has been a downward path to social instability. When the family structure unravels, adolescents in particular find that, as a result of their family's breakup, "Issues of right and wrong are open to question,"[19] thus crippling or, at least, confusing their ability to distinguish between good and bad. Once again, not all of the children of divorce, family violence, or abuse are unethical or immoral, but Wallerstein's research has shown that the devastation of the family occurring in our time poisons the root of society in undeniable ways. Because of this, a significant number of men and women in our world do not have the strength to make commitments and take moral/ethical stances that will cost them any more than they have already lost.

A TOOTHLESS LION IN THE HUNT FOR LIFE

George Gallup and Jim Castelli in their study *The People's Religion* also tell us the church is less important today. They say the church faces increasing isolation and irrelevance. Among the reasons are that people tend to see religion as a private matter, not to be influenced by religious institutions, so that a majority of us believe it is possible to be a good Christian without going to church.[20]

Furthermore, today, eighteen- to twenty-four-year-olds are most likely to say they have no religious affiliation or interest in religion; they may return to the church eventually as other generations have, but the church faces a tougher battle to reach people in the future than in the past, a problem that could be most difficult to overcome. Along with this is the reality that this generation is less likely to make commitments than any generation in modern memory. Many of today's men and women, including Christians, have decided that commitment is not in their best interests. Their primary focus is personal interest and self-preservation, so the commitment Christianity calls for is viewed less and less positively, with the result that our society will tend to become more pluralistic and less Protestant in character.[21]

Once our society was built on the bedrock of biblical revelation, but today we are building on the landfill of human wisdom, and the church is often unable to provide the support needed to protect against an ethical earthquake. In fact, the church itself has led the way into this landfill. Liberalism, brought into the church by its own seminaries, destroyed the foundation of absolute truth on which it was built, the very foundation of the identity of Christ and His power, making Him just another great historical figure (if that!). The church has become an irrelevant also-ran in the race for respect and recognition in modern society. And recently visible and influential leaders of the church have blunted its impact by disgraceful behavior. As a result, the church, once the dominant and formative influencer of our nation's values, has been elbowed aside by those espousing moral/ethical uncertainties, the absolutes of relativism.

The church is becoming the toothless lion of our times, flea-bitten and ignored in the hunt for life. Because of this, the absolute standards of biblical conviction are losing influence, and the relative standards of the general society are gaining ground. In the decade of the 1990s one expert projects that the fastest growing religions will be the non-Christian ones of Mormonism, Islam, Buddhism, and New Age sects,[22] resulting in new views of ethics that may not be compatible with what we have always held. This is particularly important in light of a developing syncretism, a "mixing and matching"[23] approach to Christianity, in which people use a spiritual grab bag to draw from other religions in order to improve one which they think is not working in their lives.

All of this, combined with a growing breakdown of stability among church leaders—the divorce rate is accelerating faster among pastors than among the general population[24]—means that the church, rather than gaining, or even holding its own, stands to lose more influence with the generation now growing up. Of course, the condition of the family is directly related to the condition of the church, and young people are coming of age without fathering either in the family or in the faith.

EDUCATION WITHOUT ETHICS

If, in our ethical ecological system, the soil of the family and the root of the church are polluted, what of the school? It would appear that the patterns established in the last twenty years will continue, making education the moral/ethical acid rain of these days. As John Silber, president of Boston University and 1990 candidate for governor of Massachusetts, sees our educational system, one of the major flaws is the breakdown of moral instruction in recent years.

> In generations past, parents were more diligent in passing on their principles and values to their children and were assisted by churches and schools that emphasized religious and moral education. In recent years, in contrast, our society has become increasingly secular, and the curriculum of the public schools has been stripped of almost all ethical content. As a result, universities must confront a student body ignorant of the evidence and arguments that underlie and support many traditional moral principles and practices.
>
> The rediscovery of the foundations of morals awaits many of the younger generation and is a major responsibility of today's educators.[25]

A public school system devoid of moral teaching and curriculum based on fundamental values is more than an educational problem. It is a workplace problem, for decisions made without a moral framework affect products, services, and the public welfare. Many graduates beyond high school—from our leading universities—lack the essentials that give them the foundation needed to make ethical decisions, or to recognize an ethical issue when they see one.

Primary factors necessary for a stable ethical foundation include a strong family influence that teaches right and wrong from childhood on, a broad training in ethical thought as seen through religion, history, and literature, and specific instruction in ethical issues themselves. When this breadth of training is missing, it becomes very difficult for the educational system to train students in ethical decision-making, since young men and women do not know how to recognize an ethical issue, as applicants for the Harvard Business School demonstrate.

In recent years, the application for admission to the Harvard Business School has been revised so it now asks questions about ethics. Among other things, the applicants must describe how they managed an ethical dilemma they have experienced. But some applicants state they have never faced an ethical dilemma. "It's amazing how many people admit they've never experienced a moral dilemma....Some [applicants] want to know if they should fabricate one," declares Laura Gordon Fisher, the Harvard Business School's admissions director.[26] It is impossible to imagine anyone bright enough and old enough to apply for the MBA program at Harvard and yet naive enough not to have faced an ethical dilemma. The only way to account for this is that the applicants, with baccalaureates from Harvard as well as other outstanding universities, are unable to recognize an issue of right and wrong because the formative elements of their growing-up years did not prepare them for ethical reality.

Deterioration in our institutions, brought about by the breakdown of the family, church, and school, which historically have provided the ethical foundation for society, has lead to a new direction in our culture. Felix G. Rohytan, senior partner at Lazard Freres & Co., says we now have a money culture. Previous generations focused on making products, but today's generation finds its driving force in *making* money and the activities related to money, according to Rohytan. Once we took pride in our products; now we take pride only in our possessions. Unless our deteriorating institutions are restored, efforts to correct the problem will be futile and ineffective.

The ethical ecological system is deeply damaged: the soil of the family lacks nutrition; the root of the church is undernourished and shriveled; the rain of the educational system is acidic and destructive.

THE MISSING LINK: NATIONAL HEROES

But what of government and its role in this personal ecological system? Here, too, there is a responsibility breakdown. Government leaders have been the inspirers of integrity and honor in our nation. People such as Patrick Henry, Benjamin Franklin, George Washington, and Abraham Lincoln have served as models to motivate generations of Americans to ethical excellence. Then came the assassination of a president, a senator and a civil rights leader in the 1960s, the self-doubt surrounding Vietnam, the stunning discoveries of Watergate, and an ongoing series of accusations against government figures. All have contributed to a now-permanent cynicism toward heroes in America. The once almost blind faith in our national institutions has been replaced by a massive distrust of all authority, especially of politicians. One poll listed the trust level of politicians as next to the bottom of the list, just one step above used car salesman. American youth coming of age in the nineties have never had heroes; they grew up cynical and have lost their capacity to make commitments. Marian Salzman, former editor of *CV*, a magazine for college students and faculty, declares:

> The twentysomething generation will do whatever they have to do to get by.... I think this is the undercommitted generation.... They don't have a passion for anything. They don't want the fast-pace rat race. They haven't bought into careers. Yuppie things don't mean much to them. They have a lack of respect for the way things have been done. They see life as a Hollywood set with nothing behind it.[27]

Certainly we should not be surprised at the fruit that our polluted ethical ecological system produces. Nor should we be surprised when some of business's brightest and best go to jail because of ethical breakdowns. We should not be surprised when educators avoid absolutes in the name of instructional equity. We should not be surprised when politicians pursue their own pleasure at the expense of the people. We should expect a tidal wave of unethical endeavors. What else can pollution produce except pollution? Has anyone ever seen a polluted river produce pure water? Can barren soil produce bountiful fruit?

The fact that barren soil cannot produce bountiful fruit brings us to the most painful reality of all in our consideration of the cause for the lapse of ethics in our time: the opportunity for fruitfulness has never been greater in history than it is in our age. In the communications area alone, we can send information almost instantly with modems, cellular phones, personal computers almost as powerful as mainframe computers, and facsimile machines, more commonly known as "fax" machines.

Technology holds the key to today's opportunity. John Naisbitt and Patricia Aburdene, coauthors of *Megatrends 2,000*, tie technology and opportunity together and tell us that telecommunications and computers will drive the change that will carry us into the new century. Tragically, the barrenness of our ethical soil may not be able to sustain us in this unmatched opportunity.

From all of this we are forced to conclude that the ecological system designed to develop moral, ethical, and spiritual people is polluted. What was once a verdant valley is becoming an encroaching desert, and each year, like the Sahara, the desert of ethical breakdown creeps further into our society, making us less and less able to discern right and wrong, let alone defend it. The inability of people to trust authority in our society, whether in government or business, means the nurturing relationships required to develop the core marks of character needed to mature leaders will not be there as they have been in the past. As a result, despite the amazing opportunities of our time for technological advancement, we run the risk that we won't have the leaders we need to take us forward to those opportunities. Again, I am not making a blanket claim, but the evidence cannot be denied: we are facing an ethical emergency that, left unchecked, will cost us the strength and stability of our society.

BEYOND THE BOTTOM LINE

*O*ur personal ecological system is polluted and our ethical foundation is flawed. We can neither grow the fruit of emotional health nor lay the strong support for the values we need to stand in today's world. In the worlds of business and politics, our nation needs a new breed of person, one who goes beyond the bottom line, who, without fanfare or personal ambition, goes about reclaiming our personal/ethical ecological system and rebuilding an ethical foundation. Such people must be men and women of courage and commitment who are willing to stand against the ethical effluence we experience today.

This book is a call to such men and women to pursue and maintain ethics based on the moral guidelines of the Holy Scriptures, to endorse ethics based on the Judeo-Christian values upon which America is founded. Such people will do more than recognize valid standards in their lives; they will motivate our youth to rise above mediocrity through the courage to commit to what is right.

Our times cry out for those who will determine to turn from the wrong, who will refuse, even in the privacy of their lives, to take the shortcut to selfishness. These will be people who define what they won't do so they can focus on what they must do. Then we will have models of moral excellence and personal sacrifice who impact others as influencers, leaders who move them toward dreams of accomplishing true greatness and deliver them from the apathy of self focus.

What does this new breed of men and women look like? They are willing to turn their corporations from seeking profit at any price to profit with dignity and concern not only for themselves but for the culture that gave birth to them. They will determine to replenish the soil that nurtured them, to return it to its pristine purity and to refresh its power and life-giving nutrients. This will make them leaders marked by integrity, intense integrity, who will not allow even the shadow of shame to touch their lives, let alone its full, deadly force.

The question is: Will *you* be such a woman? Will *you* be such a man? Will you be willing to go beyond the bottom line to the place where faith and business meet, to that place within yourself where you stand in the core of your conscience and make the decision for character rather than commissions? Will you choose for right over wrong even though such choices create opposition and stress?

Will you live out the convictions you establish alone with God day by day? Will you make the ultimate choice for God and against self? When you do, you will exhibit integrity, purity, and contentment. And then you will be the woman and the man we need to overcome the exit of ethics.

This book is a call for such men and women who will take a strong ethical stance for the good of our society. Certainly, Christians must be among those who make this decision; in fact, no Christian could ever fail to do this and honor Christ. My hope is that in the pages to follow the reader will gain insight in how to bring honor to Christ by being an ethical person in the on-going demands of daily work.

CHAPTER TWO

THE TOY CHEST

G reed is good, according to former securities trader Ivan Boesky. Speaking at the commencement of the School of Business Administration of the University of California at Berkeley in 1985, he declared, "Greed is all right, by the way. I want you to know that. I think greed is healthy. You can be greedy and still feel good about yourself."[1] In saying these words, Boesky espoused the essence of both his philosophy and his lifestyle. The most telling reality, though, is that his claim was greeted with laughter and applause. The listeners thought it was a great view of life. There was little wonder at the time that this statement was so well received.

Few have served the shrine of mammon more effectively than Ivan Boesky. In 1964, after earning a degree from the Detroit College of Law, Boesky clerked for a federal judge who was a relative of his wife. Next came a move to New York, where he served an apprenticeship in the arbitrage trade at L. F. Rothschild & Co. Boesky started his own firm in 1975, and, in 1977, he made his first big hit when he netted an estimated seven million dollars on the takeover of Babcock and Wilcox. By 1980, Boesky's capital had climbed to $90 million, and he went on to own a two-hundred-acre estate north of New York City, impressionist paintings, and a three-telephone limousine. Through large donations to Harvard University, he gained membership in the Harvard Club. He also lectured at New York University and Columbia University, though both deny his claim of academic degrees from them (published on the jacket of his book *Merger Mania*).

This guru of greed not only knew how to make millions; he could also lose millions, as he showed through major losses in 1982 and 1984. Known as "Piggy" among his peers in the arbitrage business, Boesky fell into the trap of using insider information from Dennis Levine in order to make fifty million dollars. Cornered by the Securities and Exchange Commission, he paid $100 million in penalties and ended up in prison for his crimes.[2]

Boesky might have thought greed was healthy in 1985, but what about now? Now that he has served a sentence in jail, now that he is without money, now that he is seeking to gain funds from his wealthy wife who has divorced him? Boesky has not commented on greed recently (he is not in much demand as a commencement speaker these days), so we don't know what his current feelings concerning this topic are. But we can tell that his life is not healthy—jail, divorce, and financial ruin hardly help one's welfare. Is there a better way than the greed way?

THE MOST TOYS

In the world of business, the bottom line means profit. That is essential to the health of the company, and it's an expectation of owners and stockholders alike. They are in business to make money, help the company grow, and enjoy the financial rewards of business success. There is nothing wrong with that. But always there is the danger of wanting more, of worshiping the dollar and serving it at all costs. The need for profit can become an urge for greed. And when this urge takes over, we can ignore principles of honesty, compassion, and integrity in the chase for the almighty dollar.

Whether you are an employer, management, or part of the office staff, you must fight the axiom of the marketplace: "He who has the most toys wins." This motto invades the thoughts of many executives and workers. We want a full chest of toys.

To win the game of business—and life—many think they must have the most toys, that is, the most money, the nicest house with the most "in" address, the most stylish clothes, the greatest car, the most elite corporate memberships, the biggest corner office, the most powerful position.

This is today's prevailing wisdom. But it is not accurate. The one with the most toys does not win the game of life. In fact, the person with the most toys may be life's greatest loser.

For one thing, a person can never know when he or she has won. Does it happen at age forty? Obviously not. Lots of people in business have a chestful of toys, even whole toy stores, at forty, and have empty chests at fifty. It doesn't matter whether it's forty or fifty or sixty or any age, toys have a way of slipping out of the chest, of falling out of our grasp.

The toy chest must be full, and it must have the latest and greatest diversion to be satisfying. But it never seems to stay full, as society offers newer toys for us to purchase.

We want more; there never is a final satisfaction. Oil magnate John D. Rockefeller once was asked how much money is enough. He replied, "Just a little bit more than you have."

Is there a point in life when you can say, "I've won. I quit. I am packing up my toys and going home."? Can you stop the game whenever you please? No. One of the rules of the game is you can't quit and go home while you're ahead. Everybody else wants to keep the game going, and if you don't keep playing someone else will overtake you and win. To win the game of greed and fame you must keep playing. There is no end and therefore no ultimate winner. You can lead at a certain point in the contest, but you can never be the victor.

If you join the other players in the game of greed, you can only be a winner as long as you live. Then the game ends for you; you cannot enjoy the prize. At death, he who has the most toys doesn't win. He loses. He loses all because the toys of this life are useless in the next life. Trying to gain identity in heaven from the most luxurious car on earth is like trying to win the Indy 500 with a toy model. The toys of earth are not adequate for the reality of heaven.

He who has the most toys very often loses all trying to gain all. In the tick of a second, he passes from supreme wealth to supreme poverty, from solvency to insolvency, from bounty to bankruptcy. I can think of nothing worse than to know I am going to die, realizing I must leave earth's bounty without having invested in eternity's treasures. Many will die wealthy, and yet in eternity they will have to declare bankruptcy—bankruptcy in the currency of eternal realities, not earthly resources.

BANKRUPTCY

In business, corporate or personal bankruptcy can be devastating. Your reputation is in question, your credit (initially at least) is forfeit, and daily needs become harder to meet. But eventually you can reestablish yourself; you can recover. Far worse is spiritual bankruptcy, the total loss that comes because you focused so much on the temporal that you enter eternity empty handed and stand before Christ with only ashes to show for an entire lifetime of spiritual investment.

The way to avoid spiritual bankruptcy as you enter eternity is to be certain you have made the best investments in time, the investments that Jesus Christ wants you to make with your life. People, service, and sacrifice are more important than greed and self. We must invest our energy in light of the eternal, so when we step across the line between time and eternity, we can say our lives have counted and not been wasted.

Jesus makes this point when He tells us not to lay up for ourselves "treasures upon earth where moth and rust destroy, and where thieves break in and steal," but to lay up for ourselves treasures in heaven which cannot be touched by the limitations of time (Matthew 6:19–21). Making earth's bounty our first priority on earth guarantees bankruptcy in heaven. By centering on earth's bounty we make prosperity our primary priority and seek possessions for the needs they meet in our lives. This is why we become collectors of toys; we believe they meet our deepest needs.

Three big toys tempt most of us—a home, a career, and money. Of course, having any of these is not necessarily evil or wrong. It's how we regard and treat each that affects us. As the Bible warns, "the *love* of money is a root of all evil" (1 Timothy 6:10; emphasis added), not having the money itself. When we act in greed to get more and bigger toys, those toys skew our values and move us on the road to spiritual bankruptcy. Let's look at these three big toys, and see if we are misusing them.

Do you want—or have—a large and beautiful home at the right address because the home makes you feel significant? Perhaps you want to be able to recite that address and see that everyone is impressed. You can subtly announce to the world that you are an achiever who has arrived, that you are somebody important. An address can be a passport to power, an opening in the right profession, membership in the right country club, a seat on the right board.

Maybe at this point you can't afford that grand location, but you're eyeing a move to a bigger home that includes a fireplace, swimming pool, and three-car garage. Then you can impress friends and coworkers when they visit. Either way, better location or bigger home, you crave the feeling of significance that often comes with having these things.

This feeling of significance is deceptive; we may be unaware at times that we want it. Yet some of us would consider sacrificing everything for it, even our ethics.

A second big toy can be the career we seek. For many of us, our careers are extensions of ourselves, the expression of our identity among our peers. Obviously, this is what a number of the major corporations want us to think. What could be more exciting than to have heads turn when we arrive at the office, to have others admire us and wonder about our power and influence when we move up? Like our houses, our careers can come to mean too much to us, another toy that we use to meet a fundamental need. Though this sense of identity is a distorted one, some will give up anything for it, even their families, as they channel extra hours and the best of their energies away from their spouses and children in the quest for advancement and recognition.

For some people, money is the ultimate toy, the one they must have because that's how they keep score in the game of life. More money means we're winning the game, we're superior—and superiority is what counts. Being a winner may meet one of the greatest needs some of us have, the need to be the best. Money doesn't always make us a winner, however, as a writer in the Harvard Business Review has noted.

> Money has three troublesome characteristics, and these do not ordinarily discriminate by age, gender, race, religion, national origin, or breeding. It is scarce, difficult to acquire, and transient. Before you know it, it's gone, and the less you have, the sooner you know it.[3]

Though we're aware of this, the need to win is so great in some that they'll pay any price, even their integrity, for the victory they think it brings.

We have needs for security, significance, and identity, essential needs, that drive us to become toy collectors: collectors of houses, cars, money, and much more. Those toys become most valuable to us, perhaps the most important things in our lives, because we believe they meet the most pressing needs in our lives. This means the cost of these toys can define our ethics, since what we value the most determines the price we'll pay. If we value them enough, we'll pay any price. Unless, of course, we hold certain values as absolute, a price we'll *never* pay, no matter what we face. Unfortunately, few people consistently place their deeper values above their deeper needs and wants. Do you?

THE ESSENCE OF ETHICS

That's a difficult issue to face. One way to determine what you value the most is to answer these two questions:

For what would you do anything to get?

For what would you do anything to avoid?

The answers we give to these questions establish our ethics.

For what would you do anything to get? For a house? A car? Power? Money? Whatever answer you give to this question sets the price you place on yourself, the price you place on your character, your integrity, your relationships, your family, your very life. If you are willing to do anything to obtain a goal or object, that holds greater importance in your life than such values as character and personal relationships. Some people will sell their time, their energy, and their health—even their very lives— to get what they want.

However, for many of us, our primary concern is not for what we would do anything to get. Instead, our focus is on what we would do anything to avoid. Most of us would not rob a store to get money, but would any of us break a legally binding contract if it threatened our financial resources? Many of us would not go back on a promise in order to protect ourselves, but would we keep our word if it meant losing our homes?

Ethics become an issue when what we value the most is threatened, and we must make the difficult decision of sacrificing our principles or our possessions. Ultimately, ethics are an issue of trust, a matter of which provider we will count on, mammon or God. Ethics demand a choice between masters, and the choice must be an absolute and consistent one because we cannot serve two masters[4]—we must trust one or the other; we cannot trust both, and whichever one we choose to trust replaces the other. If we choose wealth, it becomes a substitute for faith since we won't see the need to trust God.[5] Because of this, we must make the right choice, or we'll leave earth with a bounty in toys and enter heaven bankrupt in treasure. The most important decision we make in life is to make sure our death is a gain and not a loss.

A CHRISTIAN ETHIC

What does it take to make this choice between God and mammon? Our Lord's answer to this question lays the essential foundation for a Christian ethic. We must seek first God's kingdom, He says; that is, we must put God's rule and God's righteousness ahead of everything in our lives so He becomes our top priority (Matthew 6:33). To establish a Christian ethic, we must make three commitments. First, we must commit to what we will value the most, i.e., our highest priority. Second, we must commit to how we will gain what we value the most, i.e., our essential integrity. Third, we must commit to how much of earth's toys we must gain to have our needs met, i.e., our personal prosperity.

THE RIGHT PRIORITY

To practice a Christian ethic, we must first commit ourselves to the right priority, as Jesus commands when He calls us to seek God's kingdom first. This means our primary priority can be neither prosperity nor security, but obedience to God. *Seek* is a vital word in Matthew 6:33, an all-encompassing command that demands everything we are. Ours cannot be merely an intellectual commitment, but a total commitment of our emotions, our will, our aspirations, our whole being, which involves a conscious turning to God with the determined intention of obeying Him in every situation. Such a commitment means we give our hearts to God so we treasure nothing as highly as we treasure His purpose in us and in all the world. When we focus our full attention on the task of serving God, earthly toys cease to be the center of our beings.

In business, God's kingdom becomes more important than prosperity, security, promotion, or power. Service and love replace ego and superiority in the marketplace. Thus, in all our dealings we value the advance of God's kingdom before the advance of our personal kingdoms.

THE RIGHT TRUST

Second, to practice a Christian ethic, we must commit ourselves to the right trust, trust in God, that He is right in all He does and all He gives?

When we trust God, we pursue His righteousness, His view of right and wrong. His standard of moral excellence becomes our standard. We accept His definition of faithfulness in business, no matter what it costs us in terms of earth's toys. We seek security only in pursuing His righteousness, and this means a total trust in Him and His goodness.

At the center of all security is trust. So, we must decide to trust God no matter what happens, because if we refuse to trust Him none of our deepest needs will ever be met. But does trusting God and pursuing His rule and righteousness help us meet our earthly needs? Clearly yes. That's why the third element of a Christian ethic is the right provision.

THE RIGHT PROVISION

What happens to our needs for financial provision when we trust God? Some Christians wonder if God will meet their financial needs if their business ethics include a commitment to Him. The answer is yes, and the third essential element for the practice of a Christian ethic is to commit ourselves to the right provision.

This is what Jesus means when He tells us that "all these things will be added unto you" In Matthew 6:33, when Jesus speaks of "these things,"

He speaks of earthly needs such as food, drink, and clothing. The right provision is the provision God wants us to have—not what we want. We can be assured by this verse of having God's provision of treasures on earth according to His will. God will provide money, food, clothing, housing, automobiles—anything and everything that we need to pursue the priority of God's rule.

The provision of our needs comes from following the first two elements of a sound Christian ethic. In fact, the governing ethical principle for every Christian business person is this: establish the right priority and exercise the right trust, and you will receive the right provisions.

If you put God's rule first and pursue His righteousness as your primary endeavor, you will get exactly the provisions He has for you. Thus, we must be content with what God gives.

To see this principle more clearly, we look at a request addressed to God in Proverbs 30 that communicates a healthy attitude about seeking possessions.

> Two things I ask of you, O LORD;
>   do not refuse me before I die:
> Keep falsehood and lies far from me;
>   give me neither poverty nor riches,
>   but give me only my daily bread.
> Otherwise I may have too much and disown you
>   and say, 'Who is the Lord?'
> Or I may become poor and steal,
>   and so dishonor the name of my God. (vv. 30:7–9)

This prayer teaches us to respond to the urge for more in three ways.

First, we must never deceive for a profit. "Keep falsehood and lies far from me," the writer requests.

No amount of money is worth lying. If we deceive for even a dime, we make a tragic mistake that could cost us everything we hope to gain. When we lie to a customer or a supplier or an employee to get money, we show a lack of trust in God to meet our needs, and admit we have no security in life apart from money. When we lie to someone, we show that we believe the ultimate business lie: it's all up to us, and we'll never have enough unless we rely on ourselves to make it. We also believe the lie that security comes through amassing more and more; this makes money our idol. We count on it to be our peace in times of stress and our security in moments of fear.

Second, we must never reach for more than we need. "Give me neither poverty nor riches, but give me only my daily bread," the writer asks.

My father, who lived through the depths of the Great Depression, remembered one Thanksgiving when all he needed was a quarter to buy a duck. He didn't even want a turkey, just a duck. But there was no way he could get that quarter. He couldn't find enough work to earn it, and no one would lend it to him. That memory was so painful for him he never forgot it, and to this day I still remember his voice cracking with feeling as he told me about it when I was a child. He never served duck that Thanksgiving Day, and twenty-five cents remains a figure of poverty.

My in-laws worked for twenty-five cents an hour during the Depression, my father-in-law in construction and my mother-in-law as the head nurse at a small-town hospital. Those years made a deep and formative impression on them, one that molded the rest of their lives and controlled their financial decisions. Almost everyone coming out of the back-breaking poverty of the Depression, like my wife's parents, made certain they would never face such circumstances again.

Such grinding struggles scar many of us, and we determine that neither we nor our children will ever face poverty as long as we can do something about it. The urgency of this thinking may impel us to the point where avoiding poverty and accumulating wealth becomes the primary aim of our lives. Because we know we can be dominated by such an intense fear, we must do as this ancient petitioner did and ask God to deliver us from the pain of poverty.

But we must also avoid the equally destructive drive for riches. Instead, we should seek the portion God has allotted to us, the amount that will meet our needs without making us either poor or greedy. We may have to manage well; we may not have anything to spare; we may not have as much financial security as we would like; we may not be able to do some of the fun things we long to do. But we also will not be eaten alive by the driving desire to get or the terrorizing dread of losing. Instead, we'll have the peace of knowing God as our provider and the excitement of seeing how He works to meet our needs because He will indeed give us our portion, that which He lovingly intends for us.

What is my portion? There is no way we can tell in advance what God has given to us as our portion in life. I define my portion as that amount of income I can make while maintaining biblical balance in my life in the light of God's direction for me. We will discover what God's portion is for us through hard work and the exercise of the gifts and talents He has given us. God has directed some of us into pursuits that give us a lucrative income if we work with diligence and excellence. Others of us serve in fields where financial gain is not nearly as great, areas such as education, charitable institutions, or public service.

How high a price should I pay? One issue in determining what portion we should seek is how high a price we must pay for the profit we make. Often when we look at financial gain we only consider the income we make, and not the price we pay to make it. This is a mistake, because the issue is not only how much we end up with but what we pay to get it. If the cost of making money is higher than the profit we make, we are paying too high a price. If the profit costs us more than we can afford to lose, is it really a profit? I think not. In evaluating the cost of profit, we must take into consideration more than money. What about relationships, health, energy, and the intangibles that make up the total quality of our lives?

For example, suppose you choose to pursue a portion that is greater than you can get and maintain biblical balance in your life? Suppose the portion that you set for yourself costs you your wife? Suppose she leaves you, whether physically or emotionally? Suppose you wake up one day and find her missing in action, a mere shell of herself, her life gone from her, her spirit silent within her, only a deep, cold core of bitter anger where once there was the burning passion of love? If the woman you love removes herself emotionally from you, is it really a profit for you? How will you respond to the Lord when He asks you if you loved your wife as He loved you?

What if we know we're spending the assets of our wives' loyalty, love, and emotional stability to make ourselves rich? Can we dare claim we're doing this for our family? We're paying too high a price for the portion we're seeking.

And what about spiritual health? Is there no time for God? No time to pray during the day? No time to learn His Word so we can know how we can go beyond the bottom line, how we can have a faith that carries us past short-term gains to eternal returns? No time to serve others? All of this shows that we're paying too high a price for the portion we're seeking.

How can we determine our portion? Our portion is the profit we can make as we honor God by loving our mates, nurturing our children, taking care of our bodies, and trusting God for our security. It's the profit we can make even as we grow in our spirit as well as in body, mind, and emotion. Our portion is the product of hard work, a commitment to excellence, and a trust that strives to obey God in every relationship, decision, and action. Anything else means we are reaching for more than our portion.

Third, we must always be satisfied with what God provides. "Otherwise," as Proverbs 30:9 says, we "may have too much and disown [God] and say, 'Who is the Lord?' Or [we] may become poor and steal, and so dishonor the name of... God." If we gain more than our portion, we run the risk of becoming our own god, of owning so much we disown the true God by saying, "Who is the Lord?" Or, if we have too little, we may become dissatisfied and want more.

When we have hardships and depend on others, such realities of life drive us to God and a reliance on Him. But when we have more than enough, we can feel all powerful. We may think we are brilliant because people listen to us with interest. In truth, they listen to us only because money talks, and everyone listens to money. We may think we are powerful because people do what we want, but typically they obey and serve only because our money controls their responses. We think we have friends because people want to be with us. But they only want to be with us because of what we can do for them with our money. Some will please us in hopes that our influence and their association with us will advance their cause.

But if we lose our money, what happens? Our phone calls are unanswered; our commands are unheard; our friends are unavailable. Just as we must work to avoid poverty and its pain lest we become thieves, so we must avoid chasing riches that are not our portion lest we become arrogant, self-reliant gods in our own eyes. If we want to be God's men and women, we must pursue God's portion by using our gifts, our time, and our energy to work our hardest and let Him give us what He wants us to have. We cannot make money our security; instead we must trust God for our portion. And, if God gives us more than what we need, our task is to manage our money God's way according to God's standards.

The Proverbs 30 prayer is as modern as today's business page. Somewhere, on the business page of some newspaper, is a headline report about someone who deceived or deliberately confused or committed a crime, all to get more than he needed. The temptation is great. It seems so easy. Deceit and lies are committed every day by men and women who are pillars in the community, whose names are listed on the gala programs, whom politicians squire and boards recruit. The power of greed pulls the strongest down to ruin. Their shame becomes public, their names, once their honor, become notorious in their community. Never make money so important to you that you will disobey God to get it.

PROVISION, NOT PROSPERITY
PROSPERITY THEOLOGY

But what do these words from Proverbs say about the teaching that has often been called "prosperity theology"? Some argue that the faithful should have luxury automobiles, mansions, and fortunes because this is what God wants for all His children. Everyone who trusts God should have an abundance of prosperity, according to some preachers. Is prosperity God's portion for all of us?

THE WHITE CADILLAC

Those who propound prosperity theology say, "Go down and lay hands on the white Cadillac and claim it for yourself. It's yours because God wants you to have an abundance of wealth. Anyone who is truly trusting God will be wealthy. If you're not wealthy, it's because you aren't trusting God and His promises." Often the listener is asked to show he is trusting God and His promises by giving generously to the cause that the particular speaker is propounding.

In effect, we are being told to buy God's favor. The preacher might as well say, "Buy God off. Bribe Him." It's as though God sells Himself to the highest bidder. But God shows no favoritism; nor does He reward particular deeds, for He is a God of grace, not works. Nothing could be more demeaning or dishonoring to God than the prosperity gospel that claims God rewards our grandiose dreams if we just have faith.

Many of the examples in this book are of people who have obeyed God and prospered, because doing business with honesty, integrity, and quality often does produce a profit. Others, however, have been committed to honesty, integrity, and quality and have faced hard times and painful losses. There is no guarantee that God will make wealthy those who obey Him in their business endeavors. But He does promise to meet all their needs (Philippians 4:19) while building character in them. Hardships will come to all, but God sustains every believer, and those who suffer can become comforters for others who pass through hard times (2 Corinthians 2:3-4).

What God does guarantee is an eternal profit with all temporal needs met. Anything more comes as a gift of grace which demands a careful and faithful stewardship.

PROVISION THEOLOGY

We must reject prosperity theology in favor of provision theology, the fact that God will meet all our needs according to His faithful purposes and loving concern. It is our needs that are guaranteed, not our excesses, according to Philippians 4:19. We shall have "toys" here on earth. What father doesn't want to give his children toys? But it is the unwise father who gives his children more toys than are good for them, and God is not an unwise Father. So God will give us our allotted share of material goods, a share which will at least meet our needs in accordance with His most kind intentions.

For this reason we can say that if we will look out for God's interests He will look out for our needs. Provision theology says that if we will trust God for our portion, doing nothing deceptive or false, we'll have what we need. We will come to the end of life with our every need met, with all we must have to cover every obligation and die peacefully with integrity. This is God's guarantee to those who trust him.

GRACE OVER GREED

We must choose provision over prosperity, grace over greed. If, instead, we choose toys one thing is certain: we'll loose our toys. This is reality: choose toys, loose toys.

But what if we've already chosen toys? What if we've already chosen prosperity without considering the possibility that God may have a different level of provision for us? What if we've already bowed to the shrine of the god of greed, and now we have discovered the grief that greed brings? There is one hope for us: the grace of God.

Consider Bob Johnson (not his real name), who agreed to co-sign on $100 million of debt and in so doing chose to disobey God. Later he found grace not only to turn from his wrong decision but to exercise integrity in the eyes of his most intense critics, his bankers. Bob had been in the real estate business seven years when he decided to go independent, financed by a partner from one of the wealthiest families in his town, the scion to a major fortune who attracted lenders with the snap of his fingers. Could anyone be in a more enviable position? Because of his partner, Bob was finally free to use his abilities to build a superlative staff and put together a fully integrated apartment development company.

Through this company, he pursued syndication, construction, and management with a number of other outfits in his area. By the midpoint of the boom time of 1983, when real estate in his part of the world was better than it had ever been, Bob had properties going up-up-up in value. Those were the days when a developer could either buy and sell land for a profit or build and sell buildings for a profit. It was almost too easy; money could be had from banks, insurance companies, and especially from S&Ls with no effort at all.

But after three years of partnership, late in 1983, Bob began to develop an unexplainable burden, a vague uneasiness he could not escape. "I had never had so much financial success and fun, but I began to develop a burden which I didn't understand. I couldn't put my finger on it, so I took a weekend with my wife to pray and be in the Word and try to figure it all out." Despite his income and the fun he was having, he knew his partner was not committed to the same values he was because he had no commitment to Christ. At the beginning of the partnership, Bob had set it up so that all his companies were separate from his partner and he was only signing the guarantees or acting as a "banker" for him.

Later he realized this was a compromise, a rationalization, a way of massaging the facts to satisfy Scripture and justify a favorable opportunity for him.

Bob knew his partner's personal life wasn't ideal, and he "had a spiritual burden for the man," so he visited his [partner, who we'll call William]. Bob talked to William about his plan to separate the companies and Bob's future plans. He left "feeling free from my struggle, and I was sure I had done the right thing."

Two weeks later, however, his burden came back, and Bob began to lose sleep. He thought the problem might lay with the financial arrangements; *maybe I need to have a higher percentage of return from the business*, Bob thought. He visited Will again with a proposal that would increase Bob's share, and his partner agreed. Once again Bob left feeling good.

FACING THE FACTS

Bob's good feeling lasted for a month. Then, in early 1984, his burden returned, a continual burden that kept him awake at night. He knew in his heart that this burden concerned his behavior. He also knew that it was from the Lord, his partnership with a man of radically different beliefs had compromised his values and commitments, and that he had to get out of the deal. When that thought hit him, he answered, *Oh, no! I can't do that.* After a few days of thinking about it, he concluded, *Let me get all the projects we have going finished up by the end of the year, and then I'll be able to break loose.*

Within a short time, however, Bob felt so overwhelmed he knew he had to act, so he made an appointment with his partner for two days later. For two hours they talked. "I spoke my heart," Bob recalls. "I explained how I made the wrong decision and disobeyed God when I entered into the partnership, how it was my mistake, how we couldn't be partners anymore, how I had no idea what I would do for business, how I wasn't doing this out of selfish ambition but out of pure conviction."

"You're going to make $50 million with me," Will answered. "I don't understand."

Though Bob had no other partner or financial source, Will realized he couldn't talk Bob out of the decision. Bob was about to decide in faith to obey God.

Unfortunately, the two men were in numerous projects together at that time so they could not be totally separated. Bob tried to sell as many properties as he could, but he had to stay with it until there were buyers. People in the marketplace thought he had lost his mind. "I wondered about that myself off and on," Bob says. "The significance of the relationship, the financial clout, the lenders with whom it opened doors, the contacts it provided, all of this was gone. Only the Lord could have made me do this."

For the next two years, he had very little contact with his former partner. He was able to do some real estate development, but on a much smaller scale than before. "But then, on June 14, 1986, my phone rang with the biggest surprise of my life," Bob recalls. "My ex-partner's bankruptcy lawyers wanted to meet with me the next day. What a shock! In all our dealings, I had no indication of any kind that my partner faced a financial problem. I was still cosigner with him on $100 million worth of debt, which made me liable for all of it. It was joint and several. Both of us owed it all. What one couldn't pay, the other had to. The bankruptcy lawyers added panic to my shock when they told me that due to some dealings between a man with whom I was investing and my ex-partner, virtually all my personal money and company funds had been loaned to my partner without my knowledge.

"I had entrusted these funds to a friend of mine with whom I had been investing for quite some time and I thought he was putting them in safe places, but he had loaned them directly to my ex-partner without saying a thing about it to me. This meant that all of that money was frozen by the lenders; everything I had was gone. I was broke, and the lawyers told me I wouldn't be getting any of my money back. My company payroll bounced, a major mortgage payment bounced, and I had no cash to live on."

That night, a Christian leader was staying with him, and they prayed together and talked until early in the morning about God's hand in his life. Bob prayed for mercy from God, and he and his wife prayed frequently in the days that followed. He found himself in a place that was virtually indescribable; he was panicked, scared, overwhelmed, shocked. He spent the next two weeks day and night trying to work with his ex-partner, his lawyers, and lenders from all over the world. At the end of that time, in the middle of the night, he finally signed an agreement that allowed him to regain almost half of his money with a note for the rest.

"God had put me in a corner that I had no way out of other than absolutely totally turning to Him," Bob says. "The circumstances were so overwhelming that from a human and financial standpoint it seemed impossible to get out of this. All of my money had been taken away, I was cosigner on $100 million, personally liable for about half of it with a man who was broke, a couple of properties were already in default, and my partner wanted me to put all of them in default and not pay on any of them.

"I was so overwhelmed I couldn't think about leaving the house every morning without my wife and I getting on our knees and praying. Then I began reviewing every meeting with lawyers and financial advisors, and sorting through the strategies and the decisions that had to be made.

"I kept being reminded that if you ask the Lord for a fish, He's not going to hand you a snake [Matthew 7:10], and the Lord would bless us through this exercise. It was His plan, and He was orchestrating it and there was a reason behind it all, but at the time it was impossible to see what good could come out of it, . . . I had no hope of coming out of it with anything financially."

Bob had no idea if he would end up in bankruptcy and shame. As far as he could tell, he was going to lose everything, bankruptcy would follow, and he had no idea how he would support his family or how he could get through all of this. Even after the agreement was settled, he had to continue to work with the bankruptcy lawyers, with whom he had strong conflicts due to differences in values.

AVOIDING BANKRUPTCY

In 1985, the real estate market began to soften; in 1986, it fell to the bottom of the sea. Rents dropped, but expenses soared. Bob was forced to pay money out of his pocket to make debt service payments. At the same time, he was working with the bankruptcy lawyers. One by one, properties went into default. Lenders took an intimidating, threatening, litigious position, but Bob went to each one humbly trying to make a settlement, either by giving them the property or by selling it, or by working out something that was acceptable to them. He continued to raise additional equity, but the market only got worse and it became increasingly difficult to satisfy the lenders.

Despite all this, Bob did not have to go into bankruptcy, nor was he sued by any of the lenders. And he was finally repaid all the money owed him by his ex-partner. His ex-partner, on the other hand, lost everything he had, was investigated for financial improprieties, and spent six months in prison. There's no way for Bob to know what might have happened to him if he had continued in the partnership after 1984, but it could have only gotten worse and might have even entangled him in his ex-partner's criminal conviction. Although he knows he should never have involved himself in this partnership, he is grateful that God prompted him to get out when he did.

One thing carried Bob through all of this: God's Word, specifically Deuteronomy 8:2: "Remember how the Lord your God led you all the way in the desert these forty years, to humble you and to test you in order to know what was in your heart, whether or not you would keep his commands." This passage reaffirmed to him that God was with Him and that He was taking Him through this to make certain he would keep His commandments.

LESSON LEARNED

What did Bob learn from all of this?

"I learned that God's Word is absolute truth," he says. "I learned not to compromise it, not to rationalize it, not to interpret it for my own wants and needs. I realized God's Word is for our good. Just as I read thirteen years ago, God tells us not to enter into a partnership with someone who doesn't share my values, and I compromised. I read Amos 3:3 as I wanted to, and thirteen years later I am still struggling to extricate myself from that relationship.

"I know I was in an improper arrangement because my partner did not share my most important values with me and had a totally different perspective of how to deal with problems and obligations. I wanted to honor the debts, be forthright and honest, to be straight forward and reconcile with our creditors. But he wanted to sue, use bankruptcy laws, and use any means to fight his opponents. Because of this, his values and actions reflected on me."

When Bob met with the lenders, he was totally open with them. At first, they were suspicious, asking him questions about what he had done with his money, certain he had used every means possible to hide it from them. Once they became convinced that he had not done this, that he was sincere in wanting to do anything he could to satisfy their claims, they came to trust him and respect his essential integrity. In fact, some who do not have a faith in Christ have gone to his city's Mayor's Prayer Breakfast with him at his invitation out of regard for his character.

Today, his ordeal is over. Bob Johnson has emerged with a reputation for integrity, for making every attempt possible to keep his word, for being up-front in all his dealings. Unlike so many in similar circumstances over the past several years, Bob has turned from greed to grace. God has stood by Bob and given him the grace he needed to face his disobedience and its results so that his good name has been maintained without blemish or shame. Grace has brought pain with it, because we can never disregard God's standards without experiencing the consequences, but it has also brought protection and spiritual strength.

But grace has brought more than this. Former lenders are now sending investors to Bob to participate with him in new projects. Always known in his industry as a builder of excellent projects, Bob is finding that his reputation for integrity now brings him opportunities others will never see. Officers of lending institutions who observed Bob's actions now trust him, and they seek to help him move forward in his career. Even when we are attracted by greed and get caught in its trap, grace frees us from its grasp and restores us to God's blessing—but only when we choose grace over greed.

BEYOND THE BOTTOM LINE

*T*his chapter has included a contrast of two successful professionals, Ivan Boesky and Bob Johnson. One called greed good; the other found God's grace before the full consequences of greed totally crushed him. The only way we can escape greed's grip is to go beyond the bottom line, to uphold our faith in the business setting. Beyond the bottom line we will find the Word of God calling us away from the temporal appeal of amassing more and more instead of trusting Him for the portion He has for us.

God's Word guides us to the place of trust beyond the bottom line where we must make the ultimate choice. We can choose the temporary, false security that greed brings. Far better, though, to choose to trust God no matter how foolish that may appear. Even to some of Bob's Christian friends he seemed crazy to break a highly lucrative partnership. Yet, Bob's choice to trust God and do the "insane" was the one thing that delivered him from total shame and loss. In choosing to trust God, Bob turned from the temporal to the eternal.

Bob has lost much temporal wealth, but he has grown in the eternal riches of faith and character. His wife has stood by him, and there are many in his community who speak strongly of his integrity.

The question with which we close this chapter is this: which of the two are you? Are you an Ivan Boesky—the "greed is good" person who has shamed himself in every way possible? Or are you a Bob Johnson—the "from greed to grace" person who has found freedom by trusting God when it is deemed unwise or even insane? Only you can make this choice, a choice between trust in self or in God.

CHAPTER THREE

BEYOND THE BOTTOM LINE

Jack Turpin founded Hall•Mark Electronics in January 1962 on a shoe-string—$400 in cash and $20,000 in loans from friends. With four employees working at their headquarters near a Dallas expressway Hall•Mark had sales of $222,000. In the second year sales mushroomed to $1 million, and by the third year the sales exploded to $2.5 million.[1] Hall•Mark was an entrepreneur's dream come true.

Thirty years later Hall•Mark had become the third largest electronics distributor with headquarters in the United States, with 1,600 employees. Revenues in 1993 were $800 million, and when Avnet, Inc., purchased Hall•Mark in the spring of 1993, it created Hamilton Hall Mark; now that firm is the Number 1 electronics distributor in the nation.

But employee growth, market share, and financial profitability are not what define this company. Though making a profit and holding its own against competitors certainly are corporate goals, the strategy by which Hall•Mark achieved these goals makes it distinctive. Beyond the bottom line, where a person's faith and his business practices meet, Jack Turpin has conducted the business with spiritual choices and ethical standards clearly in view.

For Jack, there had to be more to business than pursuing the American dream, accumulating and consuming, working hard to succeed big. There was a greater God to be worshiped than the god of greed. Business demands a price and sacrifices must be made, but they must be made for the right reason and the right cause. He rejects the gods of greed, selfish ambition, fame, or even security, saying they levy too high a price. And he's right. Such gods attack families: marriages can grow cold and collapse; children may become distant, depressed, and even drug dependent. Friendships often are mere political alliances that ensure professional prestige and success. Employees and competitors are used, defeated, and humiliated, all in the name of business. Turpin believes business success does not require such losses. When one commits to the God of Christianity, He does demand certain sacrifices, but not the destructive sacrifices demanded by other gods.

Jack Turpin determined to serve God and that meant defining a business strategy marked by a care and service that honored Him. At the very beginning of Hall•Mark, even before Jack had grown in His total commitment to honor God through his business, he had a heart for the customer that was at the center of his business strategy.

"One thing I learned in my own personal selling as a man who understood technology and could sell technical products was how much I needed and wanted to know the customer. I could sell technical products because I had a keen desire to know the person to whom I was selling, to know their products, how they would use what I desired to sell them, how I could help them be successful as a result of my service to them. That's what I enjoyed the most about being in business and that's what I determined would be the foundational element in Hall•Mark when I started it."

This is a strategy that had to be infused with high ethical standards. Eventually, Turpin coupled his spiritual devotion and God's ethical standard of love with business and came up with a winning combination. How did all of this come about?

Before Turpin began Hall•Mark, his chief concern had been making a living for his family: his wife, Sally, and their three sons, Scott, Mark, and Jeff. For ten years, Jack was a marketing engineer for Westinghouse, his career interrupted during the Korean War for a tour of duty as a naval officer. Upon his return Westinghouse offered him a job in what was then a brand new industry, the field of electronics.

"There's something called electronics that's just starting in Dallas," they said to him. "We'll assign the Texas Instruments account to you and see how it goes." It went well, and soon the business under Jack's jurisdiction blossomed and grew dramatically.

THE #1 TARGET: KNOW YOUR CUSTOMER

During this time Jack learned one of his most valuable lessons about selling. Although a degree in electrical engineering from Rice University qualified him to be a design engineer, he had a greater desire to know the person to whom he was selling. Jack wanted to know his customers' requirements: how they would use what he would sell them and how he could help them optimize their goals. Others could develop and apply the technology; meeting customers' needs was what Jack Turpin wanted to do. He desired to know his customers in a most thorough manner, and this became the underlying principle he used for marketing products when he started Hall•Mark.

The electronics industry was the right industry at the right time for Jack, and his effectiveness soon caught Westinghouse's attention. They liked what he was doing, so they offered him a promotion to Baltimore. For the Turpins, however, Texas was home, and both had roots that went deep into Lone Star soil. Besides, Jack had seen some marketing ideas out in California that he was anxious to try, so Jack rejected the promotion and struck out on his own. With $20,000 loaned by friends who believed in his ideas, Turpin launched Hall•Mark.

When Hall•Mark began in 1962, there were no other major electronics distributors in the Southwest; today, it remains the only electronics distributor in the area that is rated in the top ten in sales. In the sixties the industry was concentrated in four places: southern and northern California, New England, and northern Illinois, especially Chicago. Two developments opened the doors for Turpin: the embryonic computer revolution and the developing space program. The technological needs of the computer industry and the National Aeronautics and Space Administration (NASA) created the high-tech component business as we know it today.[2] Turpin took advantage of the space program start-up by following the "NASA crescent," a sweep of cities where NASA's engineering, design, and manufacturing took place. The crescent curved southeast from St. Louis, to Dallas, Houston, Huntsville, Alabama, and finally Orlando. Within two years, Hall•Mark established itself in the Dallas, Houston, and Orlando markets, followed soon after that by Huntsville. The boom in the high-technology industry increased the electronic component needs of many businesses, and this helped Hall•Mark's growth significantly. As Turpin put it in an interview in 1986:

There was a void in the marketing of electronics distribution in the Southwest, and that's why we founded the company, ... The void was in the marketing of electrical components of a high-technology nature of the original equipment manufacturer, which was Hall•Mark's customer base. Our purpose was to serve that marketplace. You had fast-moving technology coming in as a result of the semiconductor phenomenon that then required totally new concepts in serving the customer. Our goal was to assist our customer in applying the high-tech products of the component manufacturer to meet the needs of our customer.[3]

Maintaining the focus on the customer and his need, Hall•Mark increased market penetration in each location and expanded from a regional to national corporation. Today they have plants in thirty-five cities and stock and distribute more than 70,000 different items consisting of electronic components and systems elements. Products include capacitors, connectors, computer disk drives, high-speed printers, fans, modems, motors, relays, semiconductors, and switch products.

THE ESSENCE OF SUCCESS

Hall•Mark represents a story of sales and business management success. But there's another side to this success story, a spiritual side that many in business don't even acknowledge, let alone recognize as central to finding success. But for Jack Turpin, this is the key to all he is and has done, the essence of his success. Honoring God by obeying His principles as found in the Bible is the "secret" to Turpin's success, one he will gladly share with anyone who asks. His life wasn't always committed to God, though. In his boyhood, Jack struggled as events prepared him for God's work in his life.

At age eleven, after his father had left because of divorce and his mother suffered poor health that kept her from working, Jack became the sole provider for the family. For four years, he ran a paper route that helped to meet the family's needs while he pursued his education. Through the influence of his fifth grade teacher, Miss Lannes Smith, Jack learned the disciplines of study, lessons that would prepare him for the world of opportunity.

Jack actually became a Christian at age eleven, just as the stress of his family was crashing in on him. Tom Shipp, youth director of Highland Park Methodist Church, took an interest in Jack and his boyhood buddies. He coached their softball team, built a relationship, and often asked them, "Are you sure you're going to heaven?" The key for Jack was that Tom lived his faith, and the reality of his commitment attracted Jack who was looking for such an anchor in his life. Gradually, he came to understand who Jesus is and made a commitment to Him that has grown to be the deepest drive of his life. Although he did not understand what he had done nor receive much help in his spiritual development for years to come, he did grow up with the conviction that a man reaps what he sows. He learned this as he watched his father's life fall apart and experienced the painful fruit that this brought into his own life. As a result, he was highly influenced by a daily fear of God and entered into the process of attempting to know Him.

TENNIS, ANYONE

At the same time that he was taking his first faltering steps of faith, he was also discovering another great love in his life, tennis. The elementary school he attended had two tennis courts, though Jack, who loved all sports, spent most of his time shooting hoops. He was not a tennis player, but found an old racket which he used to hit balls against a brick wall adjacent to the courts. One day a twelve-year-old friend, wanting someone to play tennis with, began to teach Jack the game. This boy was good for his age, so the younger Jack was trained well from the beginning. Thus Jack Turpin found his ticket out of the pain of a shattered family and his avenue into the vital relationships he would need to succeed throughout his life.

God would use tennis to open up the doors he required to get started in business, then to bring him to the place of understanding his faith more completely, and, finally, as one of the major means to help others know God as he has since come to know Him.

With Miss Smith's help and encouragement, Jack advanced in school, driven by the realization that if he was to make it in life, he needed an education. By the time Jack completed high school, he had determined his life's goals. He aimed to have the two things he had never had, a family and money. The break up of his family caused him much emotional pain, and he had spent years scrimping to meet the needs of both himself and his mother. He would have the family he missed and the money he lacked. These goals became his life's aim.

To have money, however, he needed an education, but that seemed financially impossible. No one in his family had ever graduated from college; only one family member even went to college, and that was for just one year. The only way Jack could get the education necessary to attain the goals he so badly wanted was through an athletic scholarship. Because of this, he pursued tennis as if it were his life jacket on a sinking ship. And this effort paid off.

"When I graduated from high school, I got an athletic scholarship from one of the finest engineering schools in the Southwest, Rice University in Houston. It was at Rice that I met Jess Neely, the football coach and athletic director and another of the major influences in my life. I was trying to play both basketball and tennis, and Coach Neely encouraged me to drop other sports and concentrate on tennis. He even arranged for me to have special opportunities for practice which resulted in my first national title during my sophomore year."

Other state titles followed, twenty in all. At graduation in 1952 he had an opportunity to fulfill his dream of a financially and emotionally secure family. Jack married Sally Poe, who he met four years earlier through a tennis match, and set out to get a job that would eventually pay him the grand sum of $10,000 a year, his ultimate dream salary. When Westinghouse offered him a job, he began to realize his dreams.

But a key part of life was missing. In the following years Jack's faith was real but remained static. He has always had a love for children and a desire to help them grow into healthy adults, and tennis gave him many opportunities to speak to them. Often in these times he talked about the Ten Commandments, using the game of tennis and its rules as a springboard into God's rules for life. But he lacked a deeper understanding of Scripture. During the mid-sixties, Jack met a superlative communicator who taught Bible classes for businessmen in Dallas and Austin. Exposure to this teaching sparked Jack's interest in the Bible and led him to a more serious study through the teaching of Donald K. Campbell, later president of Dallas Theological Seminary.

Jack now moved from a general knowledge of spiritual truth to a greater pursuit of biblical understanding. But his study of the Bible did not yet affect the way he ran his family and business life. All of this changed one rainy afternoon in Houston when Jack was sitting courtside under an umbrella waiting out a storm.

BEGINNING WITH THE BIBLE

By then, Jack's sons were teenagers and playing serious tennis. All of the family would go to tournaments to support whoever was playing. It was during one of these trips that Jack made his first truly life-impacting biblical discovery. As Jack tells it,

"It was about 1970, and we were in Houston during a tennis match for my oldest son. I was sitting under an umbrella waiting for the rain to stop and thinking about being a father of teenagers. I knew I didn't have very much more time left before they would leave home, and most of my opportunity to influence my sons directly would be over. I had to prepare them for what might be ahead of them, but I felt utterly inadequate for this task. I just didn't know how I would meet the overwhelming demands I faced in their lives as a father. They were good sons. We weren't having any problems with them or anything like that. It was just that fathering seemed like such an awesome responsibility that I didn't know how I would do it. It was because of this that I took a more serious look at the Bible. I had started attending a Bible study led by a man who had a real impact among businessmen, and this had prepared me to turn to the Bible when I had my feelings of inadequacy and uncertainty. From that point on, the Bible became a living book for me, a personal message from God to me, which became a guide for all I have done in the last twenty plus years."

For Turpin, the Bible now became more than ancient facts and interesting concepts; it became the source of insight into one of the two most important areas of his life, his family. From that moment on, Turpin attempted to live as a husband and father according to the Bible. The desire of his heart to have the family he never had and the increasing needs of his sons forced him to face his own inadequacies and brought him to the Bible's wisdom as God's truth. It was through this book that Jack fulfilled his life-long yearning for a healthy family. Today, as the grandfather of eleven, he looks back on that moment with gratitude for his own sense of limitation and fear and for what he learned about God's way to rear his children.

THE BIBLE AND BUSINESS?

But what about his business? Did he have no need for God in running Hall•Mark Electronics? The more Jack got into the Bible, the more he began to apply it to his whole life.

"The Bible started to bring everything in my life together, and I just naturally asked God how He wanted me to run my business according to His truth. It was at this time that I discovered Galatians 5:13. 'For you were called to freedom, brethren; only do not turn your freedom into an opportunity for the flesh, but through love serve one another.' That word *serve* leaped out at me because this is what I had always tried to do, serve the customer.

"This was the heart of my thinking when I started Hall•Mark, so I immediately began to work on ways to become even more effective in meeting my customers' needs because I realized this is how I could please God in business. Sometime later I returned to this passage and focused on the word *love*. Serving alone wasn't enough. Along with the serving there had to be love. That demand created a real dilemma for me. How in the world could I apply the idea of love in the marketplace? Business men and women understand love for family and love for friends, but not love for customers. I finally decided that I could speak of love as care, because care is something the business world understands. The issue then was how I could make all of this real in our company."

The question that he faced as he began his pilgrimage to go beyond the bottom line was: What does a love that serves look like in the everyday world of marketing, selling, negotiating, delivering, and strategizing? How can servant love make it in the arena of fast-paced competition?

A NEW MOTTO

Jack decided to begin by translating the strategy of serving love into terms his business associates could understand. He put the strategy onto the company motto: "Hall•Mark cares. Hall•Mark serves." To this new company motto he soon added an acronym built on the word *CARES*: customers, assets, resources, employees, and suppliers. They became the heart of the company's commitment to all of its clients and customers.

'C' represents customers—the life-blood of any business. But customers were not to be seen as simply means to a financial end or as statistics. Customers are people with spouses and children, people who have their own businesses or careers, people who have their own goals, dreams, concerns, and struggles. To truly love and serve them Hall•Mark employees needed to care for the things that concerned them as people, not just as objects of business.

Jack recalls doing business with Dorsett Electronics back in the sixties not long after Hall•Mark got started. When Dorsett faced a period of very tight money, Hall•Mark quickly became aware of Dorsett's needs and acted. Hall•Mark did three things for Dorsett: they extended them financial credit, they showed them how to acquire the components they needed in a systematic way so they could get their product out the door, and they enabled Dorsett to find creative sources of supply. As a result of Hall•Mark's care, Dorsett Electronics survived a drought of tight money and succeeded; without this support, Dorsett would not have made it.

'A' stands for assets, and they must be properly managed. But how? Jack Turpin decided that however the specifics of managing assets were carried out, the over-arching goal had to be that the company, its investors, and its customers needed to be the beneficiaries. This led to the institution of a system of inventory management that rapidly and consistently met customer needs so no customer would ever be let down. And that benefited everyone.

The 'R' in CARES refers to resources, namely financial resources invested in quality business services that establish Hall•Mark as a customer-conscious company rather than a profit-centered one. In other words, profit was generated not simply to line the pockets of investors and ensure the continuation of the company. The purpose was a higher one: to use profits to care for the needs of the customers. One way profits were put to good use was through debt management. Of course, all companies seek to manage their debt in a way that will benefit them. But Jack went further. He kept a tight rein on his debt so that the trust of its customers would never be broken by fears about the company's viability. The company wasn't first—its customers were—so its resources would be used to benefit them first.

The 'E' is for employees, and they are to be cared for as people who have value in themselves. They are to be trained and empowered and given a sense of responsibility, authority, and accountability as those who are most vital in carrying out the company strategy of caring by serving in order to meet customer needs. All employees are important and should be treated as such. How? Jack's answer was this: Employees need to be provided with opportunities to use their abilities, fulfill their dreams, rise to challenges, and meet their needs. To do this, he developed the management to be a positive-thinking, unified group with a common goal: caring and serving those under them. And it was Jack's job to make sure that the management team had their needs met as well.

Hall•Mark aims to provide an environment for each of its employees in which they have the opportunity to attain to their potential, so they are continually doing the very best they can as they grow in their character, skills, and contribution to all aspects of company health. Management seeks to take an interest in every dimension of their employees' lives: family, education, experience, goals. Hall•Mark avoids making demands on the personal aspects of life, but the human relationship between a caring boss and an employee provides a nurturing atmosphere and stimulates business growth in significant ways.

In order to help employees attain their greatest potential, Hall•Mark maintains and enforces the highest moral standards possible. The company will not tolerate alcohol, drugs, or immoral intercompany sexual relationships. An employee who struggles with alcohol is given two weeks to come to work sober on a regular basis. Drugs can neither be used nor sold in a Hall•Mark facility. And when a sexual relationship begins to impact the job (whether intercompany or not), management will confer with the individual. Employees know that management believes no one can reach full potential when involved in alcohol, drugs, or an improper sexual relationship, and those who want to live this way eventually leave the company because they have no future without changing. The top ten management people set the pattern, the fifty men and women who report to them follow their example, and this affects all 1,600.

Since they know the leadership really cares about enabling them to reach their greatest potential, and since they know the leadership doesn't believe they ever will make it to their best while pursuing such destructive practices, they either change or go. Although Hall•Mark pays for a counseling service for all employees which is totally anonymous, this is not the key to the quality of their care. Other companies, such as Johnson & Johnson, do this as well. The key to companies that avoid these kinds of problems lies in what they are, not what they do. When there is consistent commitment to a high ethical/moral standard out of a sense of care for the individual that is concerned with more than his/her bottom line value, employees respond and grow both in their personal lives as well as in their contribution to the bottom line. When a company goes below the bottom line in its model as well as its motto, it usually enhances its bottom line as well, although the concern must be genuine or the employee will feel manipulated.

Top management truly does model the company standard. There has not been a divorce at the upper level of Hall•Mark's management in over fifteen years. Few of the top management have a college degree, showing that no artificial barriers can ever keep any employee from rising as high in the corporation as commitment, dedication, hard work, and excellence will elevate an individual. Because Hall•Mark cares for employees, the company makes every effort to remove all barriers to each employee's full potential.

The last letter in CARES, 'S,' relates to suppliers. As manufacturers of the products Hall•Mark distributes, suppliers are mutual investors with the company in caring for and serving customers. They also need care—care for their companies, their employees, and their goals. A well-cared-for supplier is vital if customers, assets, and resources are to be handled well. The needs of suppliers vary with time and the circumstances they face. Hall•Mark seeks to help suppliers meet their specific needs in relation to such major concerns as market share, sales revenues, marketing expenses, product profitability, application insights. Because the needs of suppliers vary so greatly, Hall•Mark cannot meet all of them, but because they care they can strive to know each individual supplier well enough to meet selected needs.

Without a doubt, Hall•Mark cares, and not just in word only. But Hall•Mark also serves. At Hall•Mark, serving a customer is a higher calling than the servicing of a customer. All businesses provide some degree of service: they may have cordial telemarketers to handle orders, take returns on defective products and provide replacement without charge, or repair and upkeep products at a nominal fee. But Jack Turpin wanted to go further: he wanted to serve, not just provide services. He wanted his company's actions and motivations to flow out of a genuine concern for the needs and interests of customers, employees, suppliers, and investors, not simply out of a thin mask of self-interest. And that demanded self-sacrifice—a cost to the server that would benefit the served.

This is exactly what Hall•Mark did for the Dorsett Company back in the sixties when Jack hadn't been at it all that long. Wanting to serve another organization that faced a difficult strait, Hall•Mark was willing to take a risk and extend credit at a potential loss to itself. Granted, the Dorsett Company looked good: they had a good product and good people, but there still was risk involved. And even if there weren't risk, a lot of companies would have said, "That's not my problem. I need to concentrate on meeting my own needs, not on serving someone else." Yes, Hall•Mark got a return for serving, but they acted to meet Dorsett's specific needs by caring enough to know what kind of problems Dorsett faced. That's more than service; that's caring enough to be a servant, and that's what Hall•Mark seeks to be, a responsible servant to all in their sphere of responsibility.

A STRATEGY FOR SUCCESS

The motto "Hall•Mark Cares. Hall•Mark Serves." has been the company's for more than thirty years. How effective has the strategy been? From humble beginnings, the company has been very successful. In 1987, six years after Tyler Corporation, a holding company, bought Hall•Mark, Tyler's earnings were 11 percent higher than expected, due almost exclusively to unexpected achievements by Hall•Mark. Tyler insisted upon its purchase of Hall•Mark that Turpin continue to run the company, and Turpin sustained the successes: Tyler sold the company in 1988 for more than $200 million. Then, in the spring of 1993, the company was sold again, this time to Avnet, Inc., for nearly $500 million. Now known as Hamilton Hall Mark, this new corporation is the largest firm in its field, doing over two billion dollars a year in business. From $400 in 1962 to $500,000,000 in 1993. All this since Turpin released his business to God and developed the strategy of caring and serving from Scripture. It would seem that caring and serving has made good business sense.

Although Jack has long since given up ownership of the company (it has been publicly traded for several years), he believes his biblical strategy has made the difference. Jack is outspoken about his success: the Bible is his guidebook and prayer is his lifeline.

"Once I got into it, I developed an obsession for the Bible that has not wavered for over twenty years. I really think God wants us to read His book, so I made a commitment to God that I would read it cover-to-cover once every five years, and I have kept that commitment ever since. Through the Bible, I learned who I work for: God owns everything I have, and I am accountable to Him for all I do with what belongs to Him. When I realized that I am accountable to God, I got both a sense of responsibility and freedom because God has told us what He expects. He's written it down in a book. Every time I read it, I learn more about how to be accountable because the more you learn, the more you're expected to do.

"When I get an idea from the Bible I can apply to family or business, I bathe it in prayer, run it by other people to get their input, and then I put it to work. In my heart, I want to please God. This is why I read His book and why I will always strive to measure all I do by what He says."

This is not to say that all who follow these principles will be guaranteed success. Neither Jack nor I believe in a "prosperity theology," the belief that those who honor God in all things will always achieve material success, but we are convinced that dependent obedience to God can and does make a difference in all areas of life, including business. We understand the same principles can be used by others who do not see the same return, but everyone who uses these principles will end up with the peace of mind that comes from trusting God, no matter what He sovereignly wills for each of us.

Jack acknowledges that in his effort to maintain high ethical standards in leading a business he has faced continuous pressure for short-term performance rather than long-term performance. Often the immediate seemed to outweigh the enduring. "Next month's earnings and the current quarter earnings—these top the list of most finance-oriented elements in the business environment of the late eighties and early nineties. Far down the list of priorities are concerns about community service, long-term viability, sustained growth . . ."

Ethical leaders will be concerned with "such things as supplier loyalty, asset management, customer support, employee tenure . . . and product availability," Turpin says. He admits the external pressures for expediency and achieving the greatest bottom line at the sacrifice of principles have been the most difficult challenges in his career. "Personally, these ethical issues have been my greatest challenges, greatest opportunities, and the greatest frustrations in over thirty years of business leadership."

He recall one instance of such ethical pressured that occurred in the late 1980s. Hall•Mark was involved in a leveraged buyout (LBO), and as part of the selling process, the company was asked to develop a five-year plan that projected its financial future. It developed three different scenarios: (1) revenue growth as the primary emphasis, (2) absolute earnings as the primary emphasis, and (3) cash flow creation as the primary emphasis. The investment bankers who were funding the LBO looked at the three approaches and asked Jack to combine the three scenarios in order to project the best picture possible.

This request was unrealistic because it would have produced a business forecast that would be impossible to achieve. The primary issue here was truth, the most basic of all ethical concerns. Jack realized that creating a hybrid of all three scenarios could have projected a lie, since it could have presented far too optimistic a picture. An LBO based on too optimistic a picture might have created an indebtedness for the company that could have forced it to downsize radically, costing many loyal employees their jobs. Or it could have pushed the company over the brink of bankruptcy, destroying twenty-five years' worth of effort and achievement and putting everyone out of work.

Because of the issue of truth, Jack and Hall•Mark adamantly advised the financial dealers that management would endeavor to achieve any one of the three but rejected the hybrid proposal as representing a false future value of the company. Because of this firm position, the financial interest selected scenario number three, the cash flow position. The resulting interest on the part of new financial partners was enthusiastic, and all parties benefited significantly from the resulting course of action.

The cash flow scenario was achieved with multiplied investment returns to all parties. Within two years after the sale of the company, a major portion of the debt was paid off, and three years later Hall•Mark became an over-the-counter publicly traded company. At that time all the debt created by the LBO was paid off, and the company was debt free.

Throughout such pressures, Turpin remained committed to building a serving, caring company—one that emphasized customer satisfaction, strong inventory and delivery systems, responsible handling of debt through wise money management, employee productivity and longevity, and selfless service.

BEYOND THE BOTTOM LINE

*J*ack Turpin has learned the importance of going beyond the bottom line to make certain his faith and career meet with integrity. Such action requires a commitment to doing what is right the way God defines it. That's what this book is about. It's about those Christian principles that take you beyond the bottom line where many others have gone, to the place where faith and business meet. Here, at the confluence of the conscience, you meet God and make the most vital decision you will ever make—the decision to trust self or God, to do business your way or God's way.

In the pages that follow you will learn about putting into practice ethical principles, based on the Scriptures. Other businesspeople will tell their stories of how they practiced these principles in their business ventures. You will see that implementing the principles is not always easy, and sometimes costly. But you will always gain; sometimes your gain will be profit, sometimes satisfied customers, sometimes loyal customers. But, even if none of these happen, you will gain where it matters the most, in peace of mind, integrity, respect from peers and customers, and trust.

CHAPTER FOUR

PLAYING WITH POWER

We love power. We love to have it, to feel it, to exercise it, to dispense it, to deny it to others, to be independent because of it. Power appeals to us because we want to be in control of our lives. Power protects us. It keeps others from getting control of us. Power is attractive.

At times, however, power is misused and distorts who we are. Power makes us feel invulnerable, untouchable, unbeatable, like a god. This is its baser appeal, whether we get it through money or position or birth. We love power because it enables us to dominate others, to make them listen to us, to serve us, to honor us, to make us feel important. Sadly, many do not recognize its emptiness. Consider the hollow victory of King Ozymandias, better known as Ramses II of Egypt. Ages after his death a traveler found the pharaoh's tall image shattered, a stone face lying half sunk on the sand near legs of stone:

> *. . . Its sculptor well those passions read*
> *Which yet survive, stamped on these lifeless things,*

> *The hand that mocked them and the heart that fed;*
> *"My name is Ozymandias, king of kings;*
> *Look on my works, ye Mighty, and despair!"*
> *Nothing beside remains. Round the decay*
> *Of that colossal wreck, boundless and bare*
> *The long and level sands stretch far away.*[1]

We use power to keep ourselves from facing reality, from being held accountable, from acknowledging the rights of others, from being human the way the powerless are human. Power is attractive. Ozymandias shows the attractive addiction of power: "Look on my works, ye Mighty, and despair!" But the poet, Percy Bysshe Shelley, also shows us the deceptive side of power:

> *Nothing beside remains. Round the decay*
> *Of that colossal wreck, boundless and bare*
> *The long and level sands stretch far away.*

Power gives us the feeling we are above the rules, extraordinary, able to do what others cannot do. Most of all, power gives us the feeling we are eternal, that we'll never lose it, that we're different from everyone else who has ever held power, that what happened to pharaohs and emperors and presidents will never happen to us. But it can. And it does.

SHACKLED BY STRENGTH

Power is just as deceptive as it is attractive. When we have power we think we are independent, in charge of ourselves and others. Power gives us a rush, a high, the feeling that we are God in our own personal universe. But no one is God in his own universe. The idea of total power is a mirage. Those who sit in the seat of highest power find themselves so surrounded by the demands of others that they often feel powerless.

Even presidential power has its limits, as Senator Sam Nunn demonstrated in 1993 to the newly elected President Bill Clinton. The president had planned to sign a proclamation admitting homosexuals into the military, but Congress had something to say about this; eventually the president had to compromise. Former President George Bush could have saved Clinton the trouble. After his four years of power gridlock with a Democratic Congress, Bush knew well the limits of power. Senator Nunn and other congressional leaders forced President Clinton to adopt a radically different policy from the one the president proposed in the first place. Presidential power, like all forms of power, is limited power.

The most powerful sometimes find themselves shackled by their own strength. It is the deceptive dimension of power that makes it so dangerous. Dealing with power is like dealing with a plastic explosive: shake the wrong way and it blows up in your face.

The leaders of the Drexel Burnham securities firm found this out. A *Fortune* article entitled "The Last Days of Drexel Burnham," describes the reality of power's deceptiveness. Once a mighty force in the world of finance, its end came so suddenly and unexpectedly that *Fortune* asked, "How did such a powerful firm fail so fast? Arrogance, mismanagement, and a talent for making the kind of enemies who showed later to dance on its grave."

The article reports the following facts:

> At year-end 1988, Drexel Burnham had a brawny $1.4 billion in capital and 50 percent of junk bond underwriting. A year later its market share had dwindled to 38 percent, top executives were scrambling to roll over $300 million of the firm's own commercial paper, and Drexel was hemorrhaging—losing $86 million in one month alone.
>
> Did Drexel do itself in? Or was it done in? The truth is that this was a case of suicide—and murder. So potent had the firm become that employees truly believed they could do whatever they wanted without fear of retribution ... Says a former officer: "You see, we thought, 'We are invulnerable.'"[2]

Like Ozymandias, power made the people at Drexel feel invulnerable. But, like Ozymandias, the invulnerable were vanquished. Power turned out to be deceptive.

Yet power is also imperative. We must have power to live. Powerless people are demeaned and controlled without influence or impact. No one will get very far in business without power. The question is, what is the legitimate use of power?

TWO FORMS OF POWER

David McClelland, one-time professor at Harvard University, observes that power takes two forms, the adversarial and the beneficial or the personal and the social.[3] Dominance and the demand for submission scar the adversarial/personal face of power, while power's beneficial/social face pursues service and the desire to release others to be the best they can be. Those who use power in an adversarial way seek it for personal purposes, to control others for their own ends. On the other hand, those who use power in a beneficial way seek it for social purposes, to help others become the best they can be. God uses His power this way.

Many who resist the use of power do so because they see it as negative, as the search for personal aggrandizement and control over others. This is a misuse of power. I am speaking of power as the desire to influence others toward good, noble, and right aims by use of good, noble, and right means. It is the empowering of others to be and do their best at serving others. Such a leader's focus is on the agreed-upon corporate aims, not his own advancement, and the leader must make every effort to balance the legitimate tensions between corporate aims and employee interests, not always a clear or easy decision.

Power used for personal aggrandizement and advancement is an unethical use of power and is always destructive to the leader, the followers, and the company. In contrast to this, power used to influence others to become their best while striving for corporate aims is ethical if both the target and the means involved are ethical.

This is the difference between adversarial and beneficial power. Let's look at these two forms of power in action. First, we see the impact of adversarial power.

ADVERSARIAL POWER

Left to themselves, corporations become compartmentalized, self-focused vertical structures that function as fiefdoms. These fiefdoms, in turn, become power centers with people who look out for their own interests and compete for control at the expense of everyone else. For them, everyone who is not part of their kingdom is the enemy and is treated accordingly. To protect their self-interests, they erect vertical walls that block all others out and demand loyalty to their goals rather than commitment to the company mission and aims. In compartmentalized corporations, power protects department interests, controls department environment, and accomplishes department agendas.

This response brings a downward spiral of lowered productivity, poor quality, customer dissatisfaction, and revenue loss. If you are part of a department that views itself as a power center and sees power as the means to protect itself from others so it is in control of its own fate, you are somewhere on a downward spiral. Probably at the bottom.

The chart "Power Center" illustrates this downward spiral. By definition a power center is a department that views power as a means of control and focuses its energies on protecting itself. The manager of such a department uses his power to protect himself and his interests, to make

POWER CENTER

Focused on department interests

Loyal to department concerns

Protective of department needs

Distrusting of "outsiders"

Influenced by rumors and false reports

Committed to erroneous conclusions

Makers of false accusations

**Controlled by hidden/open
conflict with other departments**

Dedicated to internal competition

Drained by energy loss

Burned out by inefficiency

Hampered by lowered productivity/quality

Customer dissatisfaction

Revenue loss

himself look good and advance himself at the expense both of those who report to him and the company itself.

Notice on the chart the four fundamentals of a power-centered department. First, it *focuses on department interests.* The attitude is, "We got ours. You get yours any way you can, just as long as you don't get in our way. Because, if you do, look out." Second, it is *loyal to department concerns:* In fact, their own interests come before the corporation's interest, even to the point of sabotaging company goals to stay in control. Third, it's *protective of department needs,* whether for budget, personnel, equipment, or any other resource. Fourth, the power-centered department is *distrusting of "outsiders."* Walls are erected to keep others out, so no one on the inside trusts anyone on the outside.

In this closed, untrusting system *rumors and false reports receive attention*, as employees tend to listen selectively, and they often choose to hear more bad things that are not true than good things that are. From here the downward spiral continues: *managers and employees come to erroneous conclusions* (typically because they believe rumors and false reports, which leads to wrong inferences), they *make false accusations, and find themselves in both hidden and open conflict with other departments, and focus on harmful internal competition* as their goal of winning at all costs becomes more important than helping the company succeed.

As a result, managers and employees of the department are *drained by an energy loss, become burned out by inefficiency,* which yields *lower productivity and quality.* Finally, as this downward spiral approaches the bottom line, there is *customer dissatisfaction.* Poor quality and late deliveries destroy customer satisfaction, guarantee cancellations, and make it certain that the buyer will be unavailable the next time a sales representative comes calling. With fewer orders, there is *revenue loss.* No orders, no money. It's as simple as that.

When managers use power as a tool for control to protect their turf and drive their employees, they assure that the very thing they seek to avoid will happen: their departments will become inefficient, unproductive, miss the numbers, and gain a lot of negative attention.

Customers do not care about a corporation's internal power concerns. Instead of seeing a company vertically, customers see it horizontally—how its operations from one department to the next work together for the customer's needs. Because of their interest in a quality product, customers see a company in its productive entirety from leading to planning to managing to producing (whether manufacturing or service) to R&D to marketing to sales to shipping to delivery. The individual concerns of any of these departments mean nothing to the customer. All that matters to him is whether a quality product is delivered for the lowest price possible and all promises are kept.

Companies must learn to see themselves the way their customers see them and focus their power on meeting customer needs rather than protecting their own interests. The only way to make money is to meet customer needs, and making money is the only way to stay in business. Meeting customer needs becomes a map to the promised land of financial profit, employee stability, and stockholder satisfaction.

BENEFICIAL POWER

What does power properly used look like in business? Scott Turpin, son of Jack Turpin and vice president and director of quality management at Hamilton Hall Mark models the proper use of power as he leads the total quality management program (TQM) for the company. TQM uses power rightly, as defined earlier in this chapter: to influence others toward good, noble, and right aims by use of good, noble, and right means. This means empowering others to be and do their best at serving others. TQM demands the empowering of front-line employees to satisfy the customer, a process which must begin long before the product reaches the customer. Unless all management, from top to bottom, empowers all employees, the front-line men and women can never fully satisfy their customers.

Here's how TQM developed and works at Hamilton Hall Mark. (The process began while the firm was still Hall•Mark.)

Step 1: Hall•Mark determined to improve customer satisfaction.

To make money a company must make sales. No sales, no money. No business reality is more basic than this. To make sales, especially repeat sales, a company must satisfy its customers better than its competitors. The bottom line, as imperative as it is, becomes the way to keep the score. The real game is keeping the customer satisfied, *really* satisfied, not merely manipulated into thinking he got a good deal.

Hall•Mark began with its goal of customer satisfaction, so the starting point was actually the end point in its TQM planning. By starting at the end, Hall•Mark was able to ask itself questions that its customers ask and overcome many of its preconceived notions. The answers we get by asking these questions force us to face ourselves rather than protect ourselves. This led to the next step.

Step 2: To improve customer satisfaction, the company created a quality improvement team.

Management recognized that a total improvement in the quality of the company required total commitment at the top of the company. If a company is going to be the best at something, it must give its best. Hall•Mark chose its nine top executives to undertake quality improvements and provide a model of commitment to the other employees. The key leaders in the company focused their energy on the common goal of making money by maximizing customer satisfaction, not on seeking to control their own personal kingdoms.

Step 3: Hall•Mark delineated five key requirements.

After studying customer concerns, the quality improvement team determined that to optimize customer satisfaction the company had to meet five key requirements:

1. Product quality. The quality of the product itself had to meet and exceed the customer's requirements.
2. On-time delivery. The team defined on-time delivery as no days late and up to three days early.
3. Accurate shipments. The correct quantities of correct parts with the correct paperwork had to be delivered undamaged to the correct address, every time.
4. Inventory availability. The product the customer needed should be in inventory.
5. Professional service. A standard of excellence will give customers a sense of security and trust toward Hall•Mark. This would be achieved by consistently providing professional service during thousands of daily moment-of-truth interactions with customers.

Two words summarize the five requirements: reliable and responsive. Reliability and responsiveness mean customers can count on Hall•Mark to keep its promises and respond to customer needs in a timely and quality way. Further, these five requirements focus all of Hall•Mark's energy on serving the customer, not on internal warfare.

Step 4: Hall•Mark defined a specific strategy.

Without a strategy there is no progress. In their strategy, the company decided to work from the inside out to develop customer sensitivity. The leadership decided that each department should see itself as suppliers and treat all other departments as customers. As suppliers, they provide service, and this is how they measure themselves. In serving customers, they must act to meet their needs, so they serve with sensitivity. The leadership determined to make serving, not controlling, the primary aim of every department and every employee.

This step removes at least some of the possibility of internal competition and tears down at least some elements of the vertical walls. In fact, these problems will always exist no matter what strategy is employed due to the realities of human nature. Nonetheless, there has been change, and far more "Hall•Markers" see themselves the same way their customers see them, as a system of inter-related interdependent horizontal structures working together toward the same goal.

The Hall•Mark strategy demands that they serve all customers perfectly. Their stated standard of customer service is that their customers' ability to compete will be unharmed because of them. To meet this standard, employees must control cost, speed, and integrity. Hall•Mark determined to serve their customers for the least cost possible at the highest speed excellence allows and with the greatest integrity achievable. As a result, they aim to get the product to the customer for the lowest price at the earliest date with every promise kept.

Step 5: Hall•Mark listened to its customers.

You can't meet a need unless you can hear a request, and you can't hear unless you listen. The only way Hall•Mark could know what its customers needed was to ask them, which is exactly what the quality improvement team did. Through a survey and subsequent focus groups with customers, Hall•Mark determined what their needs were and established systems to meet these needs. Just by taking the step of asking its customers what they needed established the company as unique and confirmed their desire to serve them.

Step 6: Hall•Mark inculcated internal standards throughout the company.

Excellence comes from the inside out. Unless there are standards of excellence in the company, no excellence will come out of the company. For the company to achieve excellence, each employee has to be striving for it. This meant that every employee had to develop a set of five essential skills: (1) *measurement* skills that show when excellence has been achieved; (2) *goal-setting* skills that establish how much work can be done in what amount of time; (3) *teamwork* skills that make each department a work-together unit rather than competitively disunited; (4) *problem identification, analysis, and solving* skills that help each employee recognize and correct difficulties before they become big and costly; and (5) *communications* skills that enable everyone to understand each other's needs, interests, and concerns, and to work together more effectively.

Through these skills internal standards of excellence are met and maintained with a minimum of control. Rather than kill individual initiative, the training in these skills guarantees that each employee will show initiative on the task at hand. This means that employees will focus on finding, defining, and solving problems on their own rather than letting mistakes go by because that's not their job. Equipped employees are responsible employees and responsible employees are excellent employees.

Step 7: Hall•Mark required suppliers to meet stated requirements.

If suppliers don't meet your needs, you can't meet your customers' needs. Hall•Mark knew that and determined that the company would turn to its suppliers and inform them of their needs. The electronics industry is a fast-paced, constantly changing industry, and a number of Hall•Mark's suppliers did not have a customer mentality toward their distributors, including Hall•Mark. Because of this attitude, suppliers were reluctant at first to meet the new demands made of them. However, as the quality improvement team showed them how much their business would be helped by on-time delivery with a service mentality, they responded, found Hall•Mark to be right, and gratefully began to meet the new demands made of them.

With these steps, Hall•Mark was well on its way to achieving a higher level of customer satisfaction. Only two steps remained, and these involved the commitment of employees and management alike.

Step 8: Hall•Mark educated all its employees concerning the new Hall•Marker.

An educated employee is a committed employee. People who are told what to do without being told why only work for you at best. People who are told what to do without being trained don't work for you at all; they work against you.

Change cannot come by fiat. For this reason, Hall•Mark invested 16,000 man hours in education helping their employees grow in their commitment and dedication to a new mentality. This mentality, a customer/supplier/service mentality, moves departments from competition to cooperation as they develop a serving perspective. Such education brings a new loyalty to the company mission, which keeps competition where it belongs: on the street head-to-head with other electronics distributors and not in-house with other departments.

The overall educational aim was to equip Hall•Markers to understand and then work toward reaching a zero defects level in customer service. Each employee was taught "process thinking," that is, learning to think in terms of steps which lead to excellence. To accomplish this way of thinking, every employee must diligently pursue the goal of understanding his/her work requirements and then focus on making no mistakes. But no mistakes cannot mean no risk, since risk taking is essential to giving initiative to employees. The education of all employees included clear measuring standards so each one could evaluate product quality right down to the cause of a mistake and not just the symptom. The quality improvement team at Hall•Mark has discovered that the question "why" must be asked five times in order to find out what made something go wrong. Only then will the root cause of the breakdown in quality be discovered.

Educating employees in both process and problem solving, the company saw its workers change from an inspective attitude to a preventive attitude. When production is an employee's only responsibility and quality is someone else's concern, that employee will inevitably count on someone else to discover mistakes. In contrast, when the employee owns both productivity and quality, he will work to prevent mistakes at the point of production.

That's what happened at Hall•Mark, and over time the company has been able to reduce its number of quality inspectors from nineteen to four. Now employees feel both trusted and empowered. Hall•Mark uses the power it has as the employer to release the employees to contribute to the company, not to control them out of disrespect. Instead, respect replaced distrust. This level of respect has helped to lower employee turnover substantially, from more than 30 percent in 1988 (the norm for the electronics industry) to less than 15 percent in 1992. The result: Hall•Mark saved millions of dollars in hiring and training money in their work force of 1,600. Using power the right way makes great economic sense for Hall•Mark.

Step 9: Hall•Mark called for management commitment.

Unless the people at the top model the mission, the people at the bottom will miss it. For this reason, the top management of Hall•Mark were organized into the quality improvement team that established a mission statement and quality policy. Their task was to listen and understand the desires of both their customers and employees and to maximize the satisfaction of both. They aim to give customer satisfaction company-wide awareness and to help everyone focus on cost, speed, and integrity. The goal was and remains to keep cost down, speed up, and promises met.

With its successful nine-step program to increase customer satisfaction, Hall•Mark demonstrates the difference between power that serves with accountability and power that controls with domination. Power centers produce distrust, competition, and conflict, which result in lowered energy, competition, and loss of productivity and quality. All of this causes customer dissatisfaction and a loss in profits.

The power that serves produces trust, reduces competition and conflict, and increases productivity and quality. This brings customer satisfaction and a maximization of profits, exactly what we should expect in light of what Jesus said about the use of power.

Of course, Jesus wasn't talking about business and customer satisfaction when He spoke of the use of power, but His teachings have relevance to excellence in business.

THE ANATOMY OF A POWER PLAY

In the midst of His ministry, Jesus responded to a power play by two of His disciples. The response gives us insights into the appropriate use of power and how it relates to business.

SELF-ADVANCEMENT

The men who followed Jesus saw power the same way many of us do —as a means to advance themselves and gain control over others. This is what made two of them approach Jesus one day and make a grab for glory at the expense of the other ten (Mark 10:35–45). There never was a more classic power play than the one these two men, the brothers James and John, made that day. For one thing, they brought their mother, Salome, with them to act as their spokesperson, although they spoke for themselves as well (see Matthew 20:20–22). Apparently she was the sister of Jesus' mother,[4] Mary, making her Jesus' aunt and them His cousins. As the only family members among the apostles, they were already on the inside track, and they decided to leverage this advantage for their own advancement.

So they came to Jesus and said to him, "Teacher, we want you to do for us whatever we ask." Jesus, surprisingly patient with such an ambitious request, heard them out. Perhaps His patience reflects his awareness that you can't get good men without some bad struggles, and the best of men are afflicted with this kind of arrogance. Their need, apparently as He saw it, was for instruction rather than rejection.

POWER POSITION

Through their power play, James and John sought greater positions. They expected Jesus to establish a political kingdom and they were like U.S. presidential campaign loyalists who signed on early, stayed through losses in New Hampshire and Iowa and then helped win the key states. Now they think Jesus is headed for office, and they came looking for their payoff. They wanted the reward they had earned. What was their reward? The two top spots, secretary of state and chief-of-staff.

POWER PRESUMPTION

Behind their power play was a power presumption. When they asked permission of Jesus to sit on His right and His left, they presumed power was theirs for the asking to be grasped and possessed, not earned through character, commitment, and love. To these two men, power was a prize to be competed for, a privilege for self and not sacrifice, a place for control and not service. Even when Jesus challenged them as to whether they can drink His cup and be baptized His way, they missed His point and assumed He meant the cup of position and the baptism of glory. Little did they know that He meant the cup of crucifixion and the baptism of death, even though He had made this clear only moments before.[5]

POWER CONFLICT

This power play led to a power conflict. When the other ten disciples heard what was going on, they coveted what James and John pursued. For Jesus, power is not control to be grasped, but service out of sacrifice. His followers must not see power the way others do. Power is not personal and adversarial, an advantage for its possessor, but a benefit to the served. Jesus tells His followers that they are not to be as the supposed rulers of the Gentiles and lord it over others. Instead, "whoever wishes to become first among you [must] be slave of all." How often have you heard the owner of the company or the president of the division or the manager of the department, say, "What do you think I am? Your slave?" The right answer is yes if you are a Jesus-style leader and you use power the Jesus way.

SERVING POWER

By no means does this deny the use of authority on the part of leaders for the benefit of their followers. In fact, it is exactly this. Our Lord deliberately chooses words that highlight the muscle side of power and the harsh side of authority when He forbids the use of "Gentile power." No one can lead without the power and authority to do so, and the issue Jesus raises is the legitimate use of power. The only legitimate use of power Jesus sanctions is the sacrificial service of a deliverer. Of course, no one in business can do what Jesus did as our deliverer, but His power perspective applies to every life situation and demonstrates the only effective use of power there is. Serve people with your power and they will never rebel against your power; use your power for yourself and sooner or later you will lose their respect and probably your position.

POWER ENERGIZES

Legitimate leaders use their power to energize their followers by serving them and enabling them to become their best. They serve them by helping them discover and develop their abilities. For instance, when a boss becomes a mentor and helps a woman find her way among the maze of the old-boy network by lending her his name and prestige while helping her understand her true capabilities, he releases that woman to become the best she can be. He also earns her eternal gratitude and the regard as well as the respect of all who recognize his fair play. Others may resent what he is doing, but if he is fair toward all there's not much they can do about it. He has used power in a Jesus way.

POWER LIFTS

Legitimate leaders use their power to serve others by calling them to higher causes, tasks, and dreams than they could accomplish on their own. They serve their followers by challenging them to strive for greater and greater goals. When a manager rallies his department to go after an impossible dream for the sake of the good the company is doing, he uses his power to draw greater energy and effort than anyone thought possible from his people. When his followers realize they have made a contribution none of them could ever imagine, when they realize he has drawn their personal best out of them, they respond with praise and thanksgiving.

Leaders know they can't do it alone. According to Kouzes and Posner, effective leaders use their power to "build teams with spirit and cohesion, teams that feel like family. They actively involve others in planning and give them discretion to make their own decisions. Leaders make others feel like owners, not hired hands."[6]

Research has proven that "the more people believe that they can influence and control the organization, the greater organizational effectiveness and member satisfaction will be [because] shared power results in higher job satisfaction and performance throughout the organization."[7] This was demonstrated in a study designed to determine which of the branch offices of a nationwide insurance company were more effective than others. Senior leadership in the company identified ten of the offices and high performers and another ten as low performers. When financial, environmental, and managerial factors were evaluated, only one conclusion could be drawn: "employee power—the sense of being able to influence what was going on in their own offices—was the most significant factor in explaining differences between high- and low-performing branch offices."[8] In other words, properly used power lifts the followers because the leader uses his power to serve his people by leading them to the highest levels conceivable. Interestingly, this is the way Jesus used His power too.

POWER HOLDS ACCOUNTABLE

Legitimate leaders use their power to serve others by holding them accountable for their growth and development. When a vice president demands accountability from a division manager who has failed to achieve appropriate agreed-upon goals, when he puts him on notice, even when he fires him for true cause, that vice president is serving his division manager. No man can reach his best, no woman can achieve her greatest, without accountability. Illegitimate leaders use their power unjustly to destroy people; legitimate leaders use their power justly to develop people. Some people don't want to be their best; some people don't want to achieve their greatest in your company; some people don't want to pursue excellence under your leadership. We use power appropriately when we use our authority to challenge, confront, and correct such people.

To use power the Jesus way is to demand the best from people without crushing them or using them or taking advantage of them. However, good never comes from misusing your power because you fail to confront those who are failing to do their very best. We use power the Jesus way when we demand the very best that God has put in those who follow us.

POWER SERVES, NOT RULES

Business provides for the economic stability of society while giving people an opportunity to make the most of their talents and skills. Jesus provides for the spiritual deliverance of people, enabling them to become the kind of men and women who can make the most of themselves. Even though business does not have the same purpose as Jesus, CEOs and managers can learn the appropriate use of power from Him. Jesus teaches that lording it over people damages and demeans them; it creates an unhealthy fear that hinders growth and generates anger. Furthermore, Jesus teaches that excessive authority produces stress and instability and destroys loyalty. The misuse of power also produces poor quality and costs the company money.

Business leaders can also learn that the power that serves rather than rules releases people to become the best they can be. The result at Hall•Mark was a dramatic decrease in employee turnover, while quality leaped forward. This happened because employees felt responsible and had a new self-respect that reflected the respect accorded them by management. Education produced personal growth, a new excellence, and a pride that has brought the greatest employee loyalty the company has ever known.

On top of that, the company makes money. Look at the difference between Hall•Mark and Drexel Burnham, where the arrogance of power combined with greed brought the company down in a year's time. Adversarial power used for the sake of self-aggrandizement without regard for company goals or customer needs exploded in the face of those who used it, resulting in their business demise.

BEYOND THE BOTTOM LINE

*T*o exercise power properly, we must go beyond the bottom line to a healthy business ethic that cares for others. We all know the axiom, "Power corrupts and absolute power corrupts absolutely." Few things are more dangerous than power, and we must wage intense inner wars to keep ourselves from making our own self-centered power plays. Power appeals to the dark side within us, to the spirit of expediency, deception, greed, and pleasure. Unless we learn to depend on the Lord within us, the corruption that power brings will overpower our good intentions and pull us down into its destructive vortex. Only the Lord within us can give us His servant heart and enable us to exercise power His way.

All of this shows that when it comes to playing with power, you have two choices. Ozymandias or Jesus. You have the power. You make the choice.

CHAPTER FIVE

WHAT'S YOUR PRICE?

P resident of one of the premier consulting firms in his industry, with years of experience under his belt, Doug Rice[1] is highly regarded by all in his field. His company, which we'll call Mansfield International, is known for quality and integrity; he has worked long and hard to maintain that reputation by hiring the best and paying the most. Doug gives his people a piece of the action, so all officers become partners in the company. As a result, these senior employees have a major stake in what happens.

Because he knows his people are good, Doug acts to implement their ideas whenever he can. So he listened with intense interest one day to a presentation of a new opportunity available to the firm. It appeared to be a solid concept that, if successful, could substantially increase Mansfield's revenue and thereby profit to the partners. Doug agreed that they should pursue this opportunity.

HIGH VALUES, HIGH RISK

Everything seemed right about the decision until two o'clock the next morning when Doug woke up thinking about the prior day's meeting.

He soon became convinced that the decision had been based on personal gain.

"The more I pondered that decision, the more I realized I had been motivated by greed. I hadn't made a decision based on the welfare of the firm, but solely because of the personal gain I would realize. And the longer I lay there awake and unable to go back to sleep, the more convinced I was I had done a wrong thing and the more certain I became that I would have to go in and change my decision first thing in the morning.

"But that meant I faced a new dilemma. How could I explain this to my partners? I knew they couldn't help feeling I was depriving them of a good opportunity for the company and for themselves by imposing my personal values on them. Was this the right thing for me to do? The more I wrestled with the situation, the more I knew I had no choice but to risk their anger by telling them I couldn't go through with the decision I made. So, after I got to the office as soon as I could that morning, I met with one of the partners to discuss my new thinking."

To Doug's amazement, the partner understood his concerns and admitted that he also had some questions about the decision. Then Doug met with another partner who listened carefully and seemed to agree with most of Doug's perspective. The third partner, however, was surprised and perplexed by Doug's wish to void the decision. Gradually, though, this partner "changed to a reasonable level of understanding." Thus the other three partners eventually agreed with Doug.

Why did Doug have to go back and say no to doing something that could make everyone a significant amount of money? Because of his values. And his values are worth it, even if it means tension inside his company. Fortunately, his concerns with the three partners was short-lived because each understood Doug's commitment to values. Having values eventually brings trust, trust brings business, and business brings profits.

Just as differences in values can cause tension within a company, so such differing perspectives can also impact customer relationships.

HIGH VALUES, LOW BIDDERS

Several years ago, one of Mansfield's primary customers (and a significant source of income for the company) decided to do business with some other consultants. The firm's internal auditors determined that the company could get the services Doug provided cheaper, so they opened bidding to other companies. Several firms bid quite low for the customer's work, but their standards of quality were rather poor.

Doug was left with another decision. "In order to compete with the price levels of these 'low bidders,' I had three options. I could lower my fees, speed up my processes, or do both, even though I knew I couldn't do any of these options and maintain quality service. I needed the income because the well-being of my company, my employees, and their families depended on this work. Besides, if I didn't have any work, I ran the risk of losing the excellent team I had spent years assembling.

"But I just couldn't do any of these things. I listened to what they said, told them I was sorry I couldn't lower my bid sufficiently to compete with the other consultants, said I would certainly be available if they ever wanted to do business with us again, and then I hustled to sell more work elsewhere."

Why did he let the account go without pursuing any of his three options? Because of his values. Doug valued his company's good reputation above income, even though it could mean not only less profit but fewer employees. His values cost him a customer and needed income and threatened the stability of his team. Doug strives to have only one price, the price of the values to which he has committed himself. Was it worth it? Let Doug answer this question.

"Two years later the technical people in this same company went to their internal auditors and told them they were coming back to us. As it turned out, they didn't save any money by using the other consultants; in fact, it cost them a lot more money to use cheaper consultants because they were more costly in the long run. Their initial price was lower, but they either increased the cost or decreased the quality, so my old clients paid more to get less."

Doug kept his values and regained his customer. As far as he is concerned, his values were worth it. But what if his client never came back?

"Well," Doug says, "it would still be worth it to me. After all, I didn't know if they would ever come back. But, no matter what, I'm not going to make promises I can't keep, set prices I can't meet, or establish deadlines I can't hit just to keep a client. I certainly don't want to lose any clients and I'll do anything I can that is honest, ethical, and legal never to lose anyone, but if I have to choose between doing what is right or keeping a customer, I am committed to choosing what is right over any other choice. I may have to work harder than I want to sometimes because of this commitment, but knowing that I'm doing what the Lord wants me to do is worth whatever price I have to pay to please Him."

So Doug will lose his customers before he will lose his values.

Doug believes and practices integrity in his business dealings. His customers can count on Doug to be true to his word, to deliver what he promises. Integrity is "a firm adherence to a code of especially moral . . . values," according to Webster's Ninth New Collegiate Dictionary. One can adhere to his values or one call sell out, overthrowing his value system when the price is high enough.

HIGH VALUES, HIGH IDEALS

Before we discuss the temptation to "sell out," abandoning our values to the highest bidder, let's clarify what values are. We can describe values in a couple of ways.

First, values are the ideals to which we dedicate our lives, those convictions for which we sacrifice our physical health, our emotional energy, and our spiritual strength to pursue. Everyone has a set of values, and values govern all we do. Values define the bottom line of our lives, our beliefs and behaviors. Indeed, values are those driving forces within us that determine all we do.

What are some values that you may pursue? Five common ones are: Prosperity, power, prestige, position, and personal peace.

A value is something to which you attach the highest level of importance and which you pursue with intense and sacrificial energy. A value becomes an idol if you choose dedication to it over dedication to God. Why does a man choose to make his family functionally fatherless so he can negotiate and close deals or make sales eighteen hours a day? The thrill of the hunt? The excitement of the chase? The glow of the close? Perhaps his drive is much less overtly selfish than this, maybe even driven by a noble intent. The man who has been poor and determined that his children will never know the pain of poverty blinds himself to the fact that he has turned financial security into an idol and now refuses to trust God to meet his needs. Even though he may act with the greatest of integrity in his business dealings, his values are distorted because he has replaced God with another source of security. And his children grow up fatherless.

The isolation and aloneness that scarred him as a child and drive him as an adult now scar his children. Just as his father, gone scratching out a living, was unable to provide the emotional support he longed for, so he is gone, working to make certain his children will never feel the way he felt. His children will not feel the pain of financial poverty, but they will feel the pain of emotional emptiness because their father is missing.

YOUR SELLING PRICE

We not only speak of values as ideals for living. A second way to speak of value is economical, to see the value of something as whatever the market will bear.

What's your price on the open market? How much does it cost to buy your body, your soul, your spirit, your life? The value you place on yourself reflects the values to which you commit yourself. If you will sell your body for immorality, your soul for financial success, and your spirit for cultural rather than radical commitment to Christ, your values are pleasure, possessions, and acceptance. It is that simple, and there is no way around it.

Consider, for example, the response of many in our culture concerning values. During a one-week period more than 2,000 Americans answered more than 1,800 questions about the beliefs they hold most deeply. In addition to this, thousands more either answered a shortened version of the questionnaire or participated in telephone interviews. The results of these responses were analyzed and published in the book *The Day America Told the Truth*. One profound insight into American values comes in chapter eight, entitled, "What Are You Willing to Do for $10 Million? For $2 Million?" The answers tell us what price we put on ourselves on the open market. Look at these conclusions.

> Sure enough, money talked to people across the country. For $10 million, one in four of us would abandon all of our friends or abandon our church. About as many would turn to prostitution for a week. Some of us would go much farther—as far as murder, changing their race, or a sex-change operation.
>
> In fact, 7 percent of us say they would murder someone for money. That's about one in every fourteen people. Whether they could actually pull the trigger is another question, but 36 million of us would be willing to consider the offer ... The results remained pretty much the same at $5 million, at $4 million, and at $3 million.
>
> Under $2 million is where we began to see a fall-off in what people are willing to do. Our price in America seems to be $2 million or thereabouts.[2]

Each of us must ask himself, *Do I have a price?* We may not like the answer. But we need to consider the question "What's our price?" from one other perspective: What does God value? When God looks at our lives, what does He most value about us? Our response to this question will help us discover whether or not the price we place on ourselves is the right price for us. To answer this question we turn to some of our Lord's last words.

VITAL VALUES

Last words are vital words. When a person knows he faces death, he speaks his heart to those who are most precious to him. Jesus is no exception to this reality, and this is why His words on the last night of his earthly life are so important.

On an early spring night Jesus left the house of friends to go with His men across Jerusalem to the Garden of Gethsemane and His betrayal. Just before departing for the garden, Jesus had His last supper with His followers in an upper room. No words could be more important to Jesus than these words. Through them He communicates what God values the most about us, and what we must value so much that we will pay any price and make any sacrifice to gain. If those values are not ours, any profit we make pursuing other values is loss. To be wealthy without possessing what God values is to be poverty stricken in what matters the most.

As usual in His teaching, Jesus uses a picture to portray His point. Through the picture of a vineyard keeper and a vine and branches, He teaches us two key essentials: that Jesus alone is the source of our greatest value and that God regards fruit as the most valuable commodity in our lives.

JESUS: THE ULTIMATE IN VALUE

"I am the true vine and my Father is the gardener," Jesus begins. Calling Himself the "true" vine, He asserts He is the real thing, the only source of value there is. Today advertisers trumpet everything from Coke to Budweiser as "the real thing," but only Jesus is genuine; only Jesus can give us what we most desperately seek. All other sources of value are inferior, demeaning, and beneath us. If we sell ourselves for the return they bring, we shortchange ourselves and devalue our lives. To count on anything or anyone other than Jesus to give us our true value means we're accepting fool's gold rather than real gold.

NO FRUIT, MORE FRUIT, MUCH FRUIT

But what does Jesus tell us this real gold is that God values so greatly about us? As He draws the picture of the vine and branches, He repeats one word six times, showing us what God values the most. Fruit. In His last earthly words, Jesus tells us that fruit is what God values in men and women. God is the diligent farmer who tends His precious vine to make certain He reaps the greatest harvest possible from its branches. "Every branch that does bear fruit he prunes so that it will be even more fruitful" (John 15:2). Jesus describes God as the Farmer who tends the branches through a process that moves from no fruit to fruit to more fruit to much fruit. What God wants from us is the greatest amount of fruit we can bear. Depending on the gifts, temperament, life experiences, and relationships which God sovereignly gives us, plus the trust which we choose to place in Him, we bear the maximum amount of fruit we can.

But what is this fruit we must value so greatly? It has three key marks. First, fruit is Christlike character, the fruit of the Spirit, produced by the Holy Spirit through our trust in Him.[3] Next, fruit is works that have an impact for Christ, bringing others to Him. Such good works reflect the life-changing influence that Christ has through us.[4] Finally, fruit is conversation, the sacrifice of praise to God, called the fruit of the lips of those who confess His name.[5] There is a connection between these three, making them a fruit cluster: Christ's character in those who value Him above all else attracts others to Him, and all involved offer the sacrifice of praise to Him.

This is what God values the most in us, what we must value the most if we are to be men and women who please Him in the business world. We pay any price to have this fruit; we accept no price for this fruit. If this is our commitment, God will work in us to move us from no fruit to maximum fruit. We, however, must respond to God's work before we can experience maximum fruit.

When we are at stage one, no fruit, God will "lift us up,"[6] put a support under us, so we can become fruitful, even as the ancient vine dressers did. When ancient vine dressers found a branch that was not bearing grapes, they took a rock or a wishbone-shaped twig and put it under the branch to support it so it could get the proper air and sunlight to become fruitful. God does not quit on us because we are unfruitful; instead, He provides us with the support to grow strong enough in our trust to become productive. Those supportive rocks and twigs may be such resources as a Christian coworker, an office Bible study, an early morning support group, a motivating pastor—any of a number of supportive people and structures that strengthen us to the point where we bear fruit.

Currently, I am experiencing such support from a group of ten men who meet weekly from 6:30 to 8:00 in the morning. We are business and professional men in our forties and early fifties of diverse backgrounds and temperaments, who are bound together by our common commitment to bear fruit for Christ. We are active in the fields of automotive accessories, advertising, accounting, banking, education, law, gas and oil, and real estate development. Each man is a leader and some are well-known in their industry. Three have grieved at the loss of loved ones in the last few years, and we have been a support for one another in these difficult moments. Some, victims of a major recession, have faced the most difficult financial stresses of their careers while others have enjoyed good economic years. At least one has experienced unjust public attack, and we have been able to encourage him with the assurance of confidentiality. A few have started new ventures, both in business and in nonprofessional ministries. One has made a life changing decision to leave full-time business and move into helping the underprivileged.

The leader of the group, an accountant, recruited the original core as well as one of the educators to be the lead Bible teacher. With a limit of only the ten who can participate, we fill the leader's family room. Because of this, we are developing a growing closeness that many men do not experience. At the heart of each man is an intense commitment to his family and a driving desire to stand for Christ in his professional pursuits. Inevitably, our directed Bible study is interrupted by spiritual wheeling and dealing as we debate what the text means, whether we truly accept it, and what it looks like when we try to live it. When time is up we pray and head off for the battles of the day. As one of our number puts it, this is our mid-week spiritual "fix."

Occasionally we vary our format and invite a guest, usually from the world of business, to interact with us on Christian values and how to live them in the marketplace. One senior executive spoke of forty years of living according to Christ's commands in the corporate world. An entrepreneur told us how he and his partner turned down hundreds of thousands of dollars in profit for a company they were selling because they had given their word to a purchaser. Within days of their oral commitment, a much better offer was made, but, even though they had not signed any agreements, they kept their word out of honor for Christ. Although they had no idea this would happen, the Lord more than made up for their loss at a later time. On a different occasion a managing partner in a major national corporation spoke to us concerning ethical codes of conduct and what happens when profits push ethics to the side. None of us liked what we heard.

In the more than three years that we have been together we have all moved in varying stages from no fruit to fruit to much fruit in the hand of the Father. Certainly we all know what God's intervention in the fruit bearing process means in our lives because we have learned that once we are bearing fruit, our Father-Farmer takes the next step: He prunes us. To prune us means that God takes away all of those things in our lives that keep us from having a focused faith in the Lord Jesus Christ.

When He prunes us, God is cutting away our dependence on the false resources that produce false fruit. That may mean the removing of a relationship that once was a supportive rock but now has become a hindrance to our growth, causing us to rely more on the person than on the Lord. That may mean a job transfer to a place where we do not know anyone else, and we are forced to find a whole new source of strength, a new church, a new small group, a new office Bible study. That could mean the loss of a job, or even a career, so we must rely on the Lord for the courage and confidence to start all over again. That may mean tough financial times due to a recession, so we can no longer count on our money for our security, but we must trust the Lord in ways we have never trusted Him before.

Although all pruning is painful, all pruning also produces fruit. If we do not value fruit as our most precious possession, we'll resent God's interference in our lives and become bitter and angry with Him. But if we value fruit more than anything else, we'll do all we can to cooperate with God in order to bear maximum fruit.

God acts sovereignly in our lives to bring us from no fruit to fruit by providing us with the support systems we need to grow stronger in our faith. God also acts sovereignly to remove life-draining dependencies that keep us from a more fruitful faith in the Lord Jesus Christ. But once we arrive at this point, God releases us to choose whether we abide in Christ or live independently of Him. All that God does in our lives works to bring us to the place of choosing to turn from all false sources of life and put our faith in the only true source of life, the True Vine. To do this, we must abide in Christ.

To abide in Christ means two things: to maintain constant connection with Him and wholly devoted dependence upon Him. However, we must remember that this abiding has nothing to do with whether or not we know Jesus. Unless you know Christ already, nothing I am saying applies to you. Abiding relates directly and only to fruit bearing. And abiding demands constant connection with Christ along with utter dependence on him.

CONNECTION AND DEPENDENCE

What do I mean by constant connection and utter dependence? Constant connection means we allow nothing to replace the Lordship of Jesus Christ in our lives; utter dependence means we allow no other power to energize and control our lives. If we value most what God values most, we will live this way daily. If we don't, we will see our lives wither away.

During my student days, my wife and I managed a two story patio-style apartment building. The owner of the building had planted ivy, which had grown to cover one of the walls on the inside of the patio. One day, as I was sweeping the second-floor balcony, I noticed a branch that had been broken off from the vine but which was still attached to the wall. It had become disconnected from the vine. The once green, lush branch was now dry, withered, and lifeless. I pulled that dead branch off the wall, dropped it on the floor, swept it up, and dumped it into the trash. It was useless.

Just as that physical branch became disconnected from the vine, so we can become disconnected from Christ, not eternally yet emotionally. Like the branch on the balcony of the apartment building, we too can wither away because we act independently of Jesus and cease to have the life of the Vine producing His fruit in and through us. What is it that disconnects us? The decision to have idols in our lives that are more important than the true God, causing us to trust ourselves to meet our needs rather than Christ.

When we choose to go our way and live for what we value rather than what God values, we cut ourselves off from the fruit-bearing life of the Vine and bear the fruit of death instead. Thus, we must choose to make the difficult decisions in life, the decisions that keep us focused on maximizing our fruitfulness so we pursue what God values, no matter how difficult a choice this is.

THE BONDAGE OF DEBT

During the mid-eighties and early nineties our nation experienced one of the worst financial crunches we have known since the Great Depression. Business leaders worth untold millions in the mid-eighties found themselves leveraged beyond their ability. For many, bankruptcy was the only way they could see out of a lifetime of bondage to debt. Tragically, Christians were among those who regarded financial achievement more valuable than keeping their word on the notes they co-signed. Many put a higher value on prosperity than on trusting God to provide for them. Because of this, they failed to maintain their integrity and keep their good name, sacrificing these on the altar of mammon. Most did not start out thinking that way, although few thought they would ever have to pay the money back. After all, business was good. Skyscrapers were growing faster than trees.

The success formula was simple and easy to follow. Find a promising piece of land, line up some partners, bounce your idea off a bank or two (or, even better, an S&L), sign the papers, and get started on digging the foundation. True, they were doing this OPM (using other people's money); the companies lacked the reserves to cover the commitment if anything went wrong; and taxpayers would have to make up the losses if they could not make them good. These realities mattered to those who co-signed the contracts, but few thought of them at the time. What could go wrong? The notes were not due for several years, and the money would be there when the time came to pay. All you had to do was hold onto the building for five years while it appreciated and you not only made your loan back, you also made a great profit for yourself. No one got hurt; everyone was helped. Ministries and charities prospered because of the generosity produced by this galloping wealth. Good Christians were doing this in a number of boom places around the country.

The lure of seemingly easy profits reminded me of halftime at a Dallas Mavericks basketball game. Sometimes at halftime the Mavericks place a plastic see-through booth at half court and invite a lucky fan to enter it. Scattered on the floor of the booth are dollar bills, many dollar bills. Once the lucky ticket holder enters, blowers turn on and the dollar bills fly in every direction. Mr. or Ms. Lucky has two minutes to grab as many of the dollar bills as possible and stuff them wherever possible. After two minutes, the blower goes off, the remaining dollars fall to the floor of the booth, the halftime entertainment is over, and one fortunate Mavericks fan goes home with a lot of extra cash.

This is the way it was for many Mr. and Ms. Luckys around the U.S. during the eighties. Some of them were just a few years out of college, and they fell into $100,000 + a year jobs, jobs that were like the Dallas Mavericks' see-through dollar-blowing booth. They thought the dollars would continue to swirl around them; they didn't know the wind-in-the-booth event existed only at halftime, because they confused the halftime entertainment with the heat of the game. Now they know what the true game is. Unfortunately, however, they are now so hurt and beat up they may never get back into the difficult game of earning a living. With their reputations gone and trust destroyed, they have retreated to the locker room hoping the trainer can tape them up and get them out on the court again.

Surprisingly, it was not only young men and women who got caught up in the excitement of the "halftime event." Many who were older, who worked long and hard and had established themselves with banks and lending institutions, fell into the trap. Some, at least, should have known better, but they chose not to pursue constant connection with Christ and desperate dependence upon him. Instead, they apparently thought they had finally gotten in the game and received what they deserved. Some were committed Christians who gave generously to many of God's causes. The pain and shame is even greater for them. How they, and we, wish they had possessed a greater understanding of true values; how we wish they had put a greater premium on being able to keep their word for Christ rather than making a fortune to give for Christ. The allure of money and what it could do disconnected many of them from commitment to God's values and his warnings against co-signing (Proverbs 6:1–5; 11:15; 17:18). Instead, they gave themselves to a self-reliant effort to build their own identity out of dollar bills.

Rather than being utterly dependent on Christ as the only One who could meet their needs and provide them with the level of living He designed for them, they chose to become desperately dependent on money and all it could do for them. Although money can do great things for us, only the Lord adds wealth without adding pain.

HAVING GOD'S VALUES WITHIN US

What practical steps can we take to make God's values our values so we produce maximum fruit? How can we go beyond the bottom line to the foundation of life where we establish our values and build our beliefs? That night as He anticipated His garden of agony, Jesus gave His disciples, and us, three steps to make us the most we can be. God has already done His part by placing all who believe in Jesus into the Vine and by pursuing the life process of pruning us all of our days. But we must take the following three steps for ourselves, staying close to Christ and depending wholly on Him for the power to maximize our potential in Him.

ABIDE IN CHRIST

First, we must abide in Christ and choose to remain within the limits of His commands, His purposes, and His will (John 15:4–5). This begins when we commit to His Lordship and determine to do only what He wants us to do, to have only what He wants us to have, to be only what He wants us to be and to release all results to Him. Job promotions come from Him; salary raises come from Him; authority and position come from Him; influence comes from Him; recognition comes from Him.

If it isn't from Him, we must not seek it because whatever He doesn't want for us, we should not want for ourselves. Character, impact for Christ, and winning others' respect for Him should control each of our decisions. Profit comes after these three commitments, and any profit that costs us fruit should be dismissed as loss. Anything that does not come through Christ is nothing, worthless in contrast to the fruit we seek.

ASK IN PRAYER

Second, we must ask in prayer, according to John 15:7–8. Prayer becomes the center of our lives, the place of peace and perspective. Jesus tells His men to find their guidelines for prayer in the Bible through abiding in Him, so the most effective praying we do comes specifically from Scripture in submission to the lordship of Christ.

We have innumerable needs to pray about and many biblical passages to draw from, but demands come up every day in the business setting, especially for those who seek to represent Christ with integrity. We need wisdom from the rising of the sun to its setting, and wisdom comes through prayer (James 1:5–8). We must have wisdom to discern ethical issues when we face them; we must have wisdom to be creative in resolving personal tensions over ethical differences when we feel them; we must have wisdom to frame our ethical solutions carefully and winsomely when we communicate them; we must have wisdom to confront appropriately in the heat of ethical dissension when we meet it. We should never see a rising sun without requesting wisdom for the ethical demands we face in the heat of the day.

We also need courage to keep the commitments we make, and few model the courage of commitment more than Nehemiah, the governor of Jerusalem under the ancient Persian despot, Artaxerxes. A secular man who never occupied a position of religious leadership, Nehemiah risked far more than his career to accomplish his aims for God; he risked his very life. Prayer was the way Nehemiah gained courage. He asked God to help him before he spoke to the king.

As an exile in Babylon, Nehemiah served as a high-level official in the king's palace. One day, a group of men, including his brother, arrived to tell him that his beloved Jerusalem remained in shambles even though a reconstruction had been under way for some time. Obviously saddened by this disturbing report, Nehemiah could not hide his feelings from the king. To be sad in the presence of the king was a capital offense, since such a response might communicate dissatisfaction with the ruler. When the king inquired as to the reason for the sadness, Nehemiah responded with a request for a release to go to Jerusalem and rebuild its walls. His was a risky request, since Artaxerxes had stopped such construction a few years before, but Nehemiah's commitment called forth the courage required to petition the king with the dream of his heart. This was just the first of a series of courageous actions he took as he faced political intrigue, military threat, internal resistance, and spiritual stress all in a day's work.

What gave Nehemiah such constant courage? Prayer. From the first to the last of his odyssey for God, Nehemiah carried on a running conversation with God, imploring Him for blessing and success. He made no moves without first praying, and then he prayed with every step he took. Surely business men and women would benefit by joining Nehemiah in prayer for the courage of day-by-day commitment.

Nehemiah is not the only secular man who can teach us about prayerfully trusting God. We all know ethical situations are tricky. Often, there are competing issues, confusing conflicts, which create complex questions without easy answers. With God's name and blessing at stake, those who worship the true God need creativity along with faith to remain true to Him. Prayer can provide us with creative solutions, as God gives us insight as we pray and reflect on His Word, the Bible.

For instance, Daniel, another secular man from the ancient world, shows us a creative way to keep God's commandments. The issue he faced hardly appears to be an ethical one, yet food was exactly that for Daniel. Just a teenager at the time we first meet him on history's pages, Daniel was an exile from Jerusalem, a prisoner of war separated from his parents and carried off in captivity to Babylon. Knowledgeable, devout, and strong, he was chosen to serve as a courtier to King Nebuchadnezzar. In order to prepare him for this task, he had to be mentally and physically at his best. Mentally this meant mastery of the wisdom of Babylon; physically this meant eating the king's finest food and drinking his best wine.

For Daniel, this created a major ethical dilemma: he could not eat the king's finest food and obey God because God had decreed certain foods were not to be eaten by his ancient people. It was a small thing, of course. He had every reason to obey the king and no reason to obey God. After all, he was far from his home and the family he would never see again, and this was due to the hand of the God for whom he was now supposed to risk his life. There was no one to hold him accountable; he was fortunate to be alive; food was so utterly unimportant. Why put his life on the line for a few unessential commands?

But Daniel dared to stand. His daring, however, was creative, not confrontive; he worked out a "deal" with the chief official overseeing his development. "Look, let me and my friends from Jerusalem eat our kind of food for ten days and see how we do and then decide what our diet should be." In his creativity, Daniel took into account the needs of his superior as well as his conviction before God. He acted in faith and, because of his faith, God granted Daniel and his friends favor, knowledge, and intelligence in their pursuits (see Daniel 1). At times, Daniel was forced to take direct stands, but it was his commitment and creativity that brought him divine favor and established him as a man who was worthy of great trust and honor from God.

Wisdom. Courage. Creativity. Modern marketplace men and women have the same exact needs as the ancient political adviser Daniel. To implement all of this we must pray for one more grace, and that is discernment. Discernment focuses wisdom, identifies the need for courage, and gives us the shrewdness to be creative. When we ask God for discernment, we ask Him for the ability to transform knowledge into action, to take what we know from God's Word as our ethical source, mix it with our technical expertise as business men and women, and enable us to pursue His values in a way that attracts others to Him. Discernment comes through knowing and obeying the Scriptures, and we are responsible to develop discernment by pursuing God's wisdom so we both know and do what He wants.[7]

ACT IN OBEDIENCE

To maintain maximum fruit we must do three things: abide in Christ, ask in prayer, and finally, act in obedience. The more we obey the Bible in wise, courageous, and creative ways, the more discerning we become about God and life. It is for this reason that we pray with an open Bible in our hands. After God has shown us what to do through His Word and in response to our prayer by His power, act. Do what Nehemiah did when he gathered up his courage and approached King Artaxerxes at the threat of his life with his specific request. Do what Daniel did when he mixed his commitment with creativity in light of his superior's need and approached him with a "deal" that would satisfy all of the interests involved. Both men acted on their prayers to obey God. This is what we need to do as well.

BEYOND THE BOTTOM LINE

*Y*ou go beyond the bottom line when you decide what your personal values are and determine that nothing else is worth as much. Decide for fruit: character, spiritual impact, and respect for Christ from those around you. Respond to God's sovereignty by committing yourself to Christ's lordship and God's purposes for you. Then implement your commitment by determining to abide in Christ, ask in prayer, and act in obedience. By doing this, you will grow maximum fruit over the course of your lifetime.

Doug Rice made this decision early on in his life as a Christian. He and his wife, Jan, determined that they would never seek to turn the profit of fruit through Christ into loss because of selfishness. No one ever does this one hundred percent of the time. All of us are tempted and struggle and fail. From these painful and difficult moments we gain the wisdom and experience to stand strong the next time we face confusing and uncertain situations. But Doug and Jan have made every effort they could to keep the commitment they made.

The Rices teach us that nothing is as valuable to us as our values. When we regard them as our most precious possessions, we earn trust from others and have the courage to hold to our highest standards. Put no price on your values, and you'll put no price on yourself. No one will be able to buy you because no one can own you once you make your values your most valuable possession. This is the commitment Doug and Jan made.

What has come of this commitment? The answer in one word: respect. Respect for a marriage that for more than thirty years has stood as a model and witness to others. Respect for their parenting that has produced two adult children with excellent marriages who now pass on the heritage they received from their parents to their own children. Respect for their leadership since Doug serves as an elder in his local church as well as a member of the board of directors of several organizations. And finally, respect for Doug as a business man who, with Jan's support, has become the president of a consulting organization known for its commitment to integrity and quality in an industry marked by cycles of boom and bust. The business world makes no exceptions for any company no matter how high its level of integrity and quality; Doug knows well the reality of a dying market and the lack of need for outside consulting. He understands what it means to work harder and harder in the down times to compete for less and less work against those who may use lower and lower ethics. Doug can be tempted and make a decision which he regrets and must retract, but he will stand by his convictions. Doug is determined to put fruit bearing ahead of face saving or profit making.

What is your price? All too often I fear mine is too low. Raise your price by raising your values. Commit yourself to grow in character, impact, and respect for Christ from those around you. Sell yourself for nothing less than this standard, no matter what it costs you. This alone is true profit. Let this alone be your price.

CHAPTER SIX

SEX IN THE OFFICE

Joe, a salesman with a technology company, is confident, assertive, and successful. Life is going his way, and his way is the right way.

Thirty-eight, handsome, well-liked, trusted for his business integrity, and active in his church, he makes a good living for his wife and three children. His rise in the corporation has been more a rocket ride than a climb, the higher-ups think highly of him, and his future looks great in every respect.

Joe has never met a problem he couldn't lick. If ever a man could be said to have his life under control, Joe is that man.

But you can hardly tell it to see him in his office today. He has canceled all appointments and one of the most important lunches of his career. He sits at his desk stunned and confused, wondering how life could take such a sudden and sharp U-turn. He feels as if he has careened off a cliff and is crashing down a hillside, about to become a ball of fire. He is going down in flames! This was not supposed to happen to him. He's the man with life under control, the man who has never met a problem he couldn't lick! How could this be happening to him?

How could what be happening to him?

Joan, a single mother and a member of his support staff, was waiting to see him when he arrived at his office earlier this morning. She had some unexpected news. Joan is pregnant. By him.

Contrary to company policy and against every commitment he's ever made, Joe had become sexually involved with Joan. He did not start out to have an affair with her. But once it started neither of them could stop, even though both felt terrible about the way they were deceiving others and disobeying their deepest instincts to do good. Certainly, neither of them planned on a pregnancy. Joe had just met a problem he couldn't lick.

CHOICES

What can I do? Tell Joan to get an abortion? Joe knew that would be the easiest thing to do. Hide the evidence and protect himself and Joan. That way, both the higher-ups in the company and his wife would never know what they had done.

But Joe knew that wouldn't work, because neither Joan nor he believe in abortion. *I won't compound the wrong by making an innocent little life pay for our actions,* Joe told himself.

Should I get a divorce? Joe knew that would be the messiest thing to do, exposing his wife and children to the deepest pain possible and jeopardizing his status in a company in which none of the corporate officers have ever been divorced and marital fidelity is assumed for all who want to reach the top.

Should I go in and tell my boss what had happened, then go home and tell my wife what I have done? That would be the hardest thing to do because there is no guarantee he still wouldn't lose his career and his marriage. He had broken corporate policy as well as his God-sworn vow of faithfulness to his wife, and neither she nor his boss will welcome what he must tell them.

What will Joe do?

Will he do the easiest, the messiest, or the hardest thing? That is difficult to say. Just because Joe and Joan do not believe in abortion doesn't mean they will choose not to do it. After all, they have already done the wrong thing by getting involved with each other.

And what about Joan? She's a working mother and a single parent of two grade school children. She cannot quit her job to take care of a baby, and she can't afford the additional child care needed to provide for a newborn. With this kind of pressure, what's to keep them from taking the expedient step of abortion in order to protect themselves and their financial security?

No matter what Joe and Joan decide to do, there is one thing we do know: in marriage, adultery is the ultimate in unethical behavior. Promises made are not kept; trust accepted is not honored. The personal, emotional, spiritual, and financial well-being of five children and one wife are threatened all because two people chose to put their pleasure ahead of their commitments and responsibilities.

One of the greatest evidences of the ethical breakdown in our time is the meltdown of marriage and sexual commitment. If we cannot keep our word concerning marriage, the most precious relationship in life, how can we be expected to keep our word concerning contracts and money. Unless, of course, contracts and money are more important to us than marriage and commitment.

But adultery isn't the only evidence of our sexual struggle. Sex in the office comes in many forms, forms such as sexual harassment or the requesting of sexual favors, whether by a manager or a subordinate, whether by those who are single or married. For this reason, we must do more than avoid adultery if we are to be sexually ethical; we must also act to establish an atmosphere of respect and purity in our places of business so we become an influence for good in a sex-saturated society. Ethics on the job also means respect for each coworker and subordinate, including employees of the opposite sex.

SEX CENTER STAGE

Our society sizzles with sex on every level, from sexual innuendo to men's clubs to supermarkets for sex. Sex is center stage in the United States, not only in theaters but in living rooms across America. Behavior we would not even talk about in our bedrooms, let alone allow into our living rooms twenty years ago, we watch on TV with hardly a second thought. Who would ever have believed that the televised nomination hearings of a Supreme Court justice would have brought into our homes such unspeakable accusations as those made against Clarence Thomas by Anita Hill? Just think of it: a nominee for the U.S. Supreme Court sitting under the blazing spotlights of national evaluation forced to defend himself against charges of sexual harassment, charges described in specific and difficult detail.[1] When it comes to sex, there is greater publicity and less intimacy than ever before.

And what is true of the home is no less true on the job. Perhaps it is more true, for the workplace has a glamor and excitement typically missing at home. There is the thrill of projects completed, and your colleagues are alert, well dressed, and friendly. In such a setting, the opposite sex often is in his or her best light, and the powerful temptation of sex is a lion on the loose. (We discuss the lure of the office place in greater detail in the section "What? Me Worry?") Add the element of control, and a boss can be tempted to maneuver himself to an affair in the workplace.

SEX IS GOD'S IDEA

Sex. What was God doing when He created it? Why would He make such a powerful monster within us? A monster that drives us to think what we do not want to think, to desire what we do not want to desire, to do what we do not want to do? Sex is a power that demands constant guard, for no force, except the will to survive, is more powerful in a human being. No drive unleashes greater energy in the human psyche; no longing makes us more vulnerable in human relationships.

Furthermore, no issue is more pertinent to ethical and spiritual health than sexuality and sexual conduct. The misuse of sex, as we learn from Joe's dilemma, has brought immense shame to those who profess the name of Christ. Is this what God intended when He created our sexual identities?

Obviously not. God has a far higher purpose for our sexuality than for it to bring us pain and shame and to maim our marriages. We must remember that sex is God's idea, that He thought of it first. Sex is good because God said so when He created us. God made us in His image, that is, male and female, which means sexuality is at the very essence of our identity. We cannot be ourselves apart from being sexual beings; we cannot be in the image of God apart from being sexual beings. Clearly, anything that enables us to be in God's image must be good, and sexuality, as well as its expression in sex, does just that.

God made us sexual beings so we can express the creativity which He planted in us; it is through sex that we are able to participate with God in the creation of human beings made in His image and His likeness. This is certainly the greatest privilege in life, the privilege of conceiving, birthing, and raising new expressions of the image of God.

But this is not the only purpose God has for sexuality and sex. Our sexuality controls all we do, so we see life through its lens. Men and women process life differently just because we are men and women, a reality which creates great tension and difficulty until we make peace with it. Thus, the differences in men and women produce diversity in perspective, emotion, and expression, bringing with it spice and specialness.

When it comes to sex, of course, there is another purpose apart from procreation and that is the purpose of intimacy, what the Bible speaks about when it tells us that the first man and woman were naked and unashamed. This physical language actually speaks of a psychological and emotional oneness and openness, a special intimacy that sex alone can express. Without sex, we could never experience the ultimate intimacy that marriage brings, the joy of knowing and being known so completely that no other human experience compares to it. Although the misuse of sex is evil, as we see from the pain and shame that Joe and Joan face, God declares sexuality and sexual intercourse to be good.

What was in God's mind when He created sex? Joy. Thrill. Oneness. Openness. Intimacy. The exciting privilege of growing together through the seasons and decades of life in ever increasing satisfaction and completion. What greater gift could God have given us?

But there are those who argue that changing times means hanging standards. In their minds, God's absolutes are no longer in force. They claim that God's standards are irrelevant and unreal. It is this philosophy that leads to the breakdown of an ethical commitment to marriage. Now people believe it is OK to make promises and not keep them, that it is OK to deceive and hurt others who are supposed to be precious to us, that it is OK to live out of control, to break trust, to disobey God.

We know we have moved from the age of absolute morals to the age of relative morals, all in the name of progress and freedom. But have we made progress and maintained freedom in our rush to relative values?

STRAIGHT SHOOTING

John Silber, writing in his work *Straight Shooting* thinks not, when he argues cogently concerning the need for absolute values. His defense for restoring absolutes is more than just "because God says so." He declares, "We all need the help of moral principles and values, not because they sound good, but because they're as real as any laws of science."[2]

This is a profound statement. Absolutes are not the whim of an angry god who puts his creatures in bondage to impersonal and unreasonable laws, nor do we hold to them solely because of the word of a loving God, though that is adequate enough in itself. God has given us absolutes because they make sense, because life makes far more sense with them than without them. We hold to absolutes because life adds up best when we live according to them.

Silber argues further that absolutes are "the accumulated wisdom of centuries of human experience."[3] Silber speaks, not from the text of inspired revelation, although this is the most trustworthy authority of all, but from the accumulated experience of human thought. Even apart from God's revelation, there is a wisdom that tells us that practices cannot be right when they produce the kind of personal, familial, and social hurt that sexual infidelity brings. There is something inherently, even absolutely, wrong about them.

Silber makes his strongest point, however, when he writes,

> There is no area of contemporary life in which misunderstanding is greater than in the area of moral education. Values are treated today as if they were merely matters of taste. This is a thorough perversion of the nature of true values. Poisoning wells is wrong because well-poisoning is incompatible with human life. It is not wrong because I place a low value on poisoning wells and decline to award it my seal of approval. And poisoning wells is not right because someone says: "I like poisoning wells. It's fun. You ought to try it sometime.[4]

To paraphrase Silber, immorality is wrong, i.e., unethical, because immorality is incompatible with healthy human living. It is not wrong because I say so but because God says so, and because healthy living says so. All human experience throughout history confirms God's standard. Immorality is not wrong because I place a low value on it any more than it is right because someone else likes it and sees it as fun. Immorality is not a matter of opinion but a matter of revelation and the pain that a rejection of that revelations brings. In other words, human experience does confirm God's revelation, and God's truth is supported by the accumulated wisdom of humanity.

Changing times do not mean changing standards, because changing times do not alter God's purposes. The more the times change, the more clearly we must understand God's purpose in all He is doing and the more strongly we must stand on the foundation of God's absolutes. This could not be any truer than in relation to our personal sexual ethics. When we realize that the sexual act is one of the most significant ways we express God's image within us and that its misuse distorts our essential nature, we must commit ourselves to obey Him for our good in this area of our lives.

Sexual purity is a fundamental expression of personal ethics, since it confirms our inner integrity and reveals the true value and respect we place on others. Such purity shows we care for others by not taking advantage of them. In the workplace this means we respect the marriage vows of others, not suggesting or entertaining thoughts of a fling. It means we respect the talents and differences of all coworkers; we will not deride, ignore, or taunt them because of gender.

On the surface, Joe looked ethical. He did all the things ethical people do. He kept his word, returned his phone calls, was always early for appointments, never promised a false delivery date, and related well to his boss. He looked in every way like a fine, upstanding, Christian business-man, the very model of what we all aspire to be.

Beneath the surface, however, lurked deception and disrespect. He broke company policy behind his superiors' backs, deceiving them. He put a fellow employee at severe risk, not only financially but personally, emo-tionally, and spiritually by using her for his own ends. He risked the finan-cial stability of five children, three of them his own and two of them the children of the woman he professed to love. He endangered the newly con-ceived life of one of God's creatures. He played the hypocrite at church. He deceived his wife in the most important of ways, thus mocking and sham-ing her.

Of course, women also face sexual temptation to compromise their values at work. For every Joe there is a Joan. For instance, if Joan wants to compromise, she could have come on to Joe, seeking to use him for her own financial advantage, personal pleasure, and emotional security, not caring at all about Joe's family and what her actions would cost them. And there could be equal responsibility, both of them using each other for their own ends.

No matter what, the result is the same. The five children suffer, Joe's wife is deceived, and Joe and Joan both lose their integrity in the eyes of their employer.

SHORT-TERM PLEASURE, LONG-TERM PAIN

The point is this: there is a total breakdown in personal ethics when there is a breach of sexual ethics. Ethics, simply put, is love, a commitment to be concerned for the well-being of others by acting to serve them and meet their needs in any way we can, even if it means personal sacrifice for us. Paul summarizes this truth well when he tells us to look out for the interests of others even as we look out for our own interests (Philippians 2:4). Ethics is being just as concerned for others as we are for ourselves, with the result that we treat them exactly as we want to be treated by them. To tell our mates that we are faithful to them while we are deceiving them is hardly the way we want to be treated by them, as Joe would clearly state if his wife were unfaithful to him. But that is not something the Joes of this world think when they get sexually involved.

The problem is that what seems so right, so good in the darkness of our selfishness becomes shameful, ugly, and evil in the light of discovery and exposure. Nothing demonstrates this reality more clearly than the misuse of sex. But this teaches us that unethical actions, whether sexual or financial or personal, always bring short-term pleasure and long-term pain.

Because this is true, we must make every effort to be sexually ethical. To do this, we need to understand two key factors: what it means to be sexually ethical and how we can act to protect our sexual ethics.

TO LOOK IS TO DO

No one is more explicit or more graphic about sexual ethics than Jesus when He declared,

> You have heard that it was said, you shall not commit adultery; but I say to you that everyone who looks on a woman to lust for her has committed adultery with her already in his heart. And if your right eye makes you stumble, tear it out, and throw it from you; for it is better for you that one of the parts of your body perish, than for your whole body to be thrown into hell. And if your right hand makes you stumble, cut it off, and throw it from you; for it is better for you that one of the parts of your body perish, than for your whole body to go into hell. (Matthew 5:27–30)

With these words, Jesus defines sexual ethics and tells us how we can protect ourselves in this explosive area of tension.

According to Jesus, we are sexually ethical when we are free from illicit and intentional sexual desires, dreams, and deeds. Sexual ethics are not a matter of mere behavior, of avoiding the physical act of adultery alone. Obedience to God never is. Sexual ethics, like all Christian obedience, is a matter of the total person, mind, emotions, and body. This is exactly His point when He carries adultery from the physical deed to the inner desire, the lustful look.

For anyone who is even remotely honest, this is an overwhelming standard. Who can possibly avoid being an adulterer? Who has not looked with lust at someone of the opposite sex? And who can stop it? The desires seem to rush upon us without warning, unwelcomed by us, when we are unwitting, certainly unwilling, for them to enter our thoughts. We make an intense commitment to be pure in mind as well as body, but we find ourselves the helpless prisoner of our passions. What chance do we have in the face of such a relentless foe? How can Jesus be so unreasonable? It is because of this that I chose the two words *illicit* and *intentional* when I defined what Jesus meant when He spoke about sexual ethics.

Jesus does not raise an unreasonable standard, one which we can never meet. Jesus is very explicit in making His point, and the key issue is that the response must be intentional, not the unwitting glance nor the unwilling desire nor the unwanted thought. The response must be illicit, the deceptive desire that leads to the destructive behavior of a Joe or Joan.

The look that Jesus describes is an intentional look, a look with a focused purpose, a look that begins the process from emotional adultery to physical adultery. It is a deliberate desire that would act if it could act. This look is not the passing glance nor the unwanted desire of unwelcome lust. Jesus is not saying that every lustful longing means adultery, but the lustful longing that takes root in the heart and bears fruit in emotional, mental, and physical adultery. This sensual desire is a form of spiritual cholesterol which results in a severe spiritual heart attack, and it requires the same kind of radical response that a physical heart attack demands. This is exactly what Jesus calls for next as He uses even more graphic language to teach us how to respond to adulterous desires.

When Jesus speaks of the right eye and the right hand, He speaks of that which is most precious to us, since, in the ancient world, the right eye and hand were considered to be the most valuable. Most people then, as now, were right-handed. This was the favored hand. In fact, the word *sinister* derives from the Latin word for *left hand,* meaning unfavorable. To be seated at the right hand of someone is the greatest honor that could be given. Obviously, this call for radical action is not to be taken literally but figuratively. Our Lord's point is clear: take whatever radical action you must to deliver yourself from the destructiveness of adulterous desires, even if it means cutting off that which is most precious to you.

WHAT? ME WORRY?

"Of course, adultery is wrong," you may say as you read these warnings. "I wouldn't commit adultery. A joke or two isn't so bad, and I really don't say anything that bothers other people. I don't have anything to worry about here." Yet, you and I may be in more danger than we realize or want to acknowledge. Many executives, managers, and other workers have fallen prey to sexual desire because of this kind of thinking—"It can't happen to me." Such a naive perspective is dangerous, for many reasons.

Each day as we go to our offices, we enter places that challenge us to excellence. We work with others in relationships of closeness and dependency. The normal demands of business mean that we spend more time with people in the office than we do with our own mates and families. Eventually a sense of intimacy can develop, and, when the relationship is with the opposite sex, it can be difficult to not think—or want—such intimacy to develop into something romantic.

Furthermore, we often see our fellow workers under better circumstances than we do our wives and husbands. We all come to the office looking our best and working our hardest. The time we spend there is often a time when we must give our best, when we are called to rise above adversity and pull together in commitment to our vision. We go into battle for the cause, fight our common competition, give all we have, and celebrate our win together. Meanwhile, our wives may be at home taking care of sick children, fighting a flooded bathroom, picking up after a two-year old, struggling to survive one more day of motherhood. Perhaps she forgets how important it is for her to look her best and be ready for the homecoming of her knight in shining armor. Or, if you're a career woman, you may find that an upper-level executive is more exciting than your husband, who may be on the road too much and seems too tired when he comes home and doesn't talk much (or listen much). Your fellow worker smiles, listens, cares, and seemingly understands.

Almost without knowing what is happening, we can fall from our perch of saintly sexual confidence into the abyss of sexual shame. There we stand in our confusion saying, "She was such a good listener," or, "He was so understanding." "I just don't understand it all. I didn't plan for this to happen." The wisest thing we can assume is that when it comes to sex, nobody's a saint because everyone's liable. Assume "I can do it" and act to protect yourself before you do something you really don't want to do.

WHY IS IT WRONG?

BAD BUSINESS

Why is it unethical to pursue sex in the office, to be the Joe and Joan of your company? If for no other reason than that sex in the office is just plain bad business. Sexual liaisons can alter relationships in the office, causing you or the other person to show favoritism, create fear, distrust, or resentment by other employees or the person you are involved with. Sexual relationships fog up the atmosphere and create confusing tensions that hinder effectiveness. This pragmatic reason alone should be enough, but there are far greater and deeper reasons why sex is not welcome in the office, and these reasons relate to why God created sex in the first place.

ULTIMATE INTIMACY

God designed sex to be the ultimate in intimacy, the most intense oneness and openness possible. In sex there is a total self-revelation, which demands maximum trust. This is the reason every culture regulates sexual relationships in some way, why the privacy of sex demands a public ceremony of covenant commitment. What we call a wedding ceremony is actually a form of a covenant initiated by God in which the participants give their word to be faithful and true to Him and to one another alone.

Such a word given in response to God initiates a trust that creates the security and stability needed for healthy sex to flourish. Sex in the office destroys this trust.

LOSS OF SECURITY

Along with intimacy, God designed sex for procreation so we could join Him in the creation process. The greatest gift a parent can give to a child is security, the sense of significance and worth that makes a child feel loved and valuable. Parents can only bless children with the gift of security if they are secure in their own relationship, and such security demands trust. Sex in the office destroys trust at home, and shattered trust at home means shattered security in children. It is unethical in the most serious way for anyone to destroy the innocent for the sake of selfish pleasure.

LOSS OF PLEASURE

God also designed sex to provide unthreatened pleasure for husband and wife, the excitement and delight of enjoying one another as created by Him. To share ourselves in uninhibited trust for the purpose of giving and experiencing unthreatened pleasure to someone who is deceiving us is to mock ourselves. Such illicit pleasure can destroy us at the very root of our personhood. Sex in the office or anywhere else outside of marriage can never give the secure joy God intended for it.

LET'S GET IT STRAIGHT: SEXUAL HARASSMENT

However, we must remember that improper sexual relationships involve more than action; it also involves unwelcome suggestions, solicitations, and assertions.

All of us can agree on the realities of improper sexual intercourse, but what about the realities of improper sexual innuendo, the gray-to-black hassle of sexual harassment? What many men think of as "just innocent fun" hits many women as discomforting invitations to unwanted involvements. A young career woman related to me the extreme distress and embarrassment she felt when a superior commented about how attractive she is on several occasions. These comments came from a Christian leader and were undoubtedly done innocently, but this illustrates how even offhanded comments can create severe tension. Both men and women must be aware of the devastating impact that such comments can have on those around them.

Let's get it straight so we know what's right. Let's define sexual harassment.

The Supreme Court in 1986 "recognized what is known as 'hostile-environment harassment'—any on-the-job sexually oriented activity that creates a hostile or offensive working environment but does not involve economic factors"[5] is sexual harassment. Conduct causing such a hostile environment involves verbal or physical behavior "that creates an intimidating, hostile, or offensive work environment or unreasonably interferes with an employee's job performance."[6] Sexual harassment occurs when an employee's employment, status, or job performance depends on responding positively to unwelcome sexual advances, requests for sexual favors, or other forms of verbal or physical conduct of a sexual nature.[7] As men and women who are committed to healthy sexual conduct, we must make every effort to avoid any word or action which even remotely approaches such harassment.

FIVE STEPS TO DELIVERANCE

What steps can we take to maintain our sexual ethics, either to prepare ourselves for a healthy sexual relationship or protect ourselves from becoming deceptive and destructive Joes and Joans? I suggest five steps for all who wish to be sexually ethical, whether married, single, or divorced, and one additional step specifically for those who are single, whether never married or previously married.

1. TRUST CHRIST

All who seek to maintain their sexual ethics need a solid foundation: we must come to Christ and trust Him for eternal life. He is the one who gives both the perspective for proper sexual behavior and the power, through the Holy Spirit, to live a strong sexual ethic.

Perhaps you have already failed to meet Christ's standard in this world of sexual activism and reaped the results of such failure. In truth, you have deceived and used one of God's children, whether a mate or office partner or someone else. You must realize that God is displeased with your misuse of the sacred trust of His image. Once you realize this and are ready to confess this sin and that you are by nature in rebellion against God, the way to spiritual salvation is easy. Jesus died for us because we are guilty of distorting God's image in some way, whether it is a breach of sexual ethics or some other act of disobedience. His death pays the price for our disobedience, and His resurrection releases us from the power and control of its grip on us.

For this reason, if we will acknowledge our wrongdoing, ask God for forgiveness on the basis of Christ's death for us, and trust Jesus for this forgiveness, we shall receive pardon for our actions, spiritual and emotional cleansing, deliverance from ultimate judgment, and eternal life. Coming to Christ in faith out of a full awareness and acknowledgment that we have wronged God and others brings freedom from past failure and a new beginning. There is no greater step we can take to wholeness than this one.

2. GIVE GOD YOUR BODY

Next, settle the basic issue of personal purity by giving your body to God to belong to Him as His living temple. Give up your own claim on your body. He created you, and therefore He owns every dimension of your life, including your body. In fact, the Scriptures say that your body "has been bought with a price," God's sacrifice of His Son, and you are to "glorify God in your body." Thus your body is not your own but belongs to God (1 Corinthians 6:19–20).

Freedom only comes from yielding every member of our physical bodies to God to be instruments for accomplishing His right purposes (Romans 6:12–13), and the decision to be pure by the power of God is the initial step toward the releasing joy of being sexually ethical.

3. DECIDE TO DENY IMMORALITY

Third, make the decision that by Christ's power you will never be involved in immorality. Willpower alone is not enough, but the absence of such a decision leaves us with no defense when illicit desire comes knocking at the door. At least a will, buttressed by the determination to obey God and disciplined to deny illicit desire, provides some resistance until we are able to marshal other spiritual, emotional, and personal forces to counterattack devious calls to disobedience.

One of the most common reasons for moral failure is the unfortunate fact that most people who are sexually unethical have never decided not to be. This leaves them without a guard at the gate when temptation comes calling, and temptation will come calling no matter what decision we make. Remember, though, that noticing an attractive member of the opposite sex is not wrong. What is wrong is to focus on that person for the purpose of pursuing sexual desire, whether in dream or deed. It is the intentional, continuing focus on lustful feelings that Jesus condemns as adultery, whether mental, emotional, or physical.

In order to implement your determination not to commit immorality, write out a covenant between you and God that will give you a permanent record of your intention as well as the date on which you made it. If you wish to, tell a trusted friend or two of your desire for true sexual freedom. You could enter into a covenant of accountability with a few friends in which you support one another in your purpose to be pure. On regular occasions, review your covenant and report to one another as to how you are progressing in your resistance to immorality.

Another reason for moral failure is that virtually all who fall have chosen not to have any form of moral accountability to help them keep the promises they make, whether to God, themselves, or their mates. Because loving and faithful friends form a fortress of support and encouragement against sexual attack, we must establish such accountability relationships. All of us need friends who mean so much to us we could not face them if we were untrue to our mates and families. We need a safe place to go with our struggles and temptations.

One way to protect ourselves is to leave a trail of accountability, a record of our daily activities. Our secretaries should always know where we are and how we can be reached; our fellow workers should know our patterns and practices, when we come, when we go, and who can reach us at essential times. Our mates need to sense our total openness with them about our schedules, and we must be comfortable with the fact that if they walked in on us at any time we would be unthreatened, unembarrassed, and innocent of all wrong doing. We will only be accountable if we choose to be, but this is one of the most important and essential choices we'll ever make in life.

4. COMMIT TO FAITHFULNESS

Fourth, commit yourself to a sexual relationship as God created and designed it to be, a permanent, monogamous marriage relationship until death do you part. If you are married, this is the commitment you made, and this is the commitment you must maintain to be faithful to your promise and your God. If you are single, this is the commitment you must plan to make in order to be healthy and whole as a human being.

One practice you might implement is to run a weekly check on your PQ, your purity quotient. At least once every week, enter into a time of prayer and evaluation concerning your personal purity, asking yourself in God's presence how your thought life is doing, how strong your resistance is to the intentional illicit look. By running a weekly check, you will be much more likely to remember your commitment before God on a daily basis, and you will see yourself make much progress toward your goal of being sexually ethical and maintaining your sexual integrity.

5. MEET YOUR MATE'S NEEDS

Here's one final point for every married man and every married woman: before God and in obedience to Him, meet your mate's sexual needs. God commands those who are married to meet each other's sexual needs without hesitancy or excuse. Many are shocked to discover that the Bible is so explicit about sex, especially when it comes to practicing sex within marriage. Although God strongly condemns sex apart from marriage, He heartily commands it in marriage. It is not just that God commends sex in marriage, as if it were a recommended practice; it is a commanded practice so that no husband or wife can be pleasing to God apart from making every effort to sexually satisfy each other.[8] Sex is not evil. As I said earlier, sex is God's idea; He thought of it first, and all that He created He called good.

Because sex is good, God commands it for husbands and wives,[9] so all who are married are commanded to meet each other's sexual needs with only one exception, and that is introduced by the words "except perhaps" (see 1 Corinthians 7:5). The exception is a mutually agreed upon time of prayer which is optional and not required. In other words, the absence of sex in a marriage relationship should be an agreed upon exception to the norm for one purpose only: the short-term pursuit of prayer, after which husband and wife return to their healthy sexual relationship.

A marriage without regular and consistent sex is not a godly marriage, but one in which there are serious and dangerous problems. It is a marriage marked by disobedience. Obviously, short-term physical limitations that require common consideration make for exceptions to this standard, but apart from unusual and debilitating physical problems, consistent sex is the biblical standard for a godly marriage.

THE SINGLE LIFE

And now six words for the single person: get pure, be pure, stay pure.

Throughout this chapter, I have been writing to the married about adultery, but it is also true that sex between an unmarried man and an unmarried woman is also outside of God's blessed intentions. The apostle Paul is clear in 1 Corinthians 6:18–20. There is no biblical exception to this standard, and all are held accountable by it. For this reason, you must first seek to be single and content. Certainly, times of dissatisfaction and intense loneliness will occur when you will long for the companionship that

God designed a sexual relationship to provide. There will be days of difficult and demanding temptation, especially when an attractive sex partner is available. But God can give you a sense of contentment which will make you a complete and healthy person without sex.

Marriage and sex may be preferable, but they are not essential for personal wholeness. More than one married person will tell you that a wrong mate is far worse than no mate. Because this is the case, take steps that will keep you out of situations that increase your dissatisfaction. Make the commitments I mentioned above: come to Christ, settle the basic issue of who owns your body, make the decision to be sexually ethical, implement it with a covenant between you and God, and involve a few trusted friends as part of your support system for sexual ethicalness. Where possible, avoid places, practices, and people that bring you into temptation or cause you to fall.

If you have never been sexually active, don't start now, no matter how great the pressure put upon you. If you have been sexually active, it will be more difficult for you to maintain your commitment, which is even more of a reason to take radical, diligent steps to protect yourself and your integrity. Unless you are desperately dedicated to contentment as a single through God's power, you will open yourself up to even greater hurt than the loneliness you feel at times now. Few things are more devastating than the wrenching loss of a sexually active relationship. However, even if you have been previously married, using sex as a single person to cure loneliness is like using alcohol to cure feelings of inferiority; all that results is worse pain than before. Apart from the commitment and wholeness of a marriage relationship, sexual intimacy can never be satisfying.

BEYOND THE BOTTOM LINE

*T*here are a lot of Joes and Joans in this world, married or single, who have pursued sexual favors or conquests in the office only to discover that such encounters bring grief into their lives. They have refused to go beyond the bottom line to uphold a sexual ethic by God's grace. Instead of standing on the rock of truth, they have settled on the sands of deception. The image of integrity and faithfulness that they so carefully constructed has crumbled. They chose self and not God; they found shame and not good.

Sex is God's idea. He thought of it first, and He designed the sex act to be a glorious and joyous expression of commitment between a husband and a wife that leads to a growing excitement and satisfaction across the years of a faithful marriage. He did not design sex to be a furtive and fleeting office flirtation that leads to the confusing and painful choices of abortion or confession or economic hardship or divorce and family destruction. Be sexually ethical by expressing your sexuality God's way.

CHAPTER SEVEN

COMING IN FIRST

Valentine's Day, 1993. Daytona Beach, Florida. A great day for the running of the Daytona 500. One of the crown jewels of automobile racing, the Daytona 500 is the Super Bowl of the NASCAR circuit.

Throughout the week leading up to this event drivers participated in qualifying rounds and preliminary races, all building up to the climax, the 500 itself. Now 150,000 fans, including 53,000 on the infield, are gathered to cheer on their favorite race team. Tickets are hard to come by and expensive—$120 face value for the best, but far more than that from the scalpers hawking their wares at the approaches to the raceway. Fans come for the sights, the sounds, the smells, the action, the thrill of it all.[1]

To win the Daytona 500 is a NASCAR driver's greatest dream, but many among the best have never won. One of these, Dale Earnhardt, a five-time Winston Cup champion, is the favorite. Despite fourteen tries, he has yet to see the checkered flag at Daytona. There are other famous names trying to complete the 500-mile course first, including the pole winner Kyle Petty, son of Richard Petty, and Dale Jarrett, son of retired NASCAR champion Ned Jarrett. Interestingly, Ned will be up in the CBS booth trying to be objective as he calls the race his son is driving.

EVERYTHING A FAN COULD WANT

The 1993 Daytona 500 may have been the best ever. This race had it all. Danger. Drama. Excitement. Everything a fan could want. Six wild crashes, all without injury, provided the danger. According to reporter Gerald Martin, one was "a gut-wrenching and barrel-rolling banger" from which, amazingly enough, the driver, Rusty Wallace, walked away.[2]

For drama, there are thirty-eight lead changes among thirteen drivers in two hundred laps. A shoving match erupts between Kyle Petty and Bobby Hillin following an accident that cost Petty an opportunity to win the $1 million winner bonus put up for him by his car owner, Felix Sabates.[3] Finally, there's one of the greatest finishes in Daytona history, a dead heat in the last lap. During that exciting final lap, Earnhardt and Jarrett race one and two. One-hundred-ninety-nine laps done, and it all comes down to the final two-and-a-half miles of the race.

Jarrett drove down inside the track as Earnhardt slid up high between turns three and four. Side-by-side they come, Earnhardt's Chevy and Jarrett's Lumina, bumping door-to-door out of turn four toward the checkered flag.[4]

Up in the TV booth, another drama was unfolding. The producer, Bob Stenner, sitting in the control truck, seeing what was happening, never hesitated. He hit everybody's key and said, "Lay out." Then he said, "Ned, root your son home. Be a father."[5] Ned dropped all semblance of objectivity and began to cheer his son home.

> Come on, Dale, go baby go. Alright, come on . . . Come on, take her to the inside, don't let him [Earnhardt] get on the inside of you . . . It's Dale and Dale as they come off Turn 4 . . . You know who I'm pulling for is Dale Jarrett . . . Bring her to the inside Dale, don't let him get down there . . . He's gonna make it, Dale's gonna win the Daytona 500. All right! . . . Look at Martha [Ned's wife] . . . Oh, can you believe it! . . .[6]

Never in history had a father called his son's winning effort.

The excitement had crested down in pit row. During the final three laps everyone on Jarrett's team was jumping up and down, cheering, praying, doing everything they could to root the "Interstate Batteries" Lumina home. Crew chief Jimmy Makar has been going to Daytona for fifteen years, but he's never won before. Today is different for him. Joe Gibbs, retired Washington Redskins coach and the owner of the car, can now boast of three National Football League Super Bowl wins and a Daytona 500 victory. After the race, he said that the triumph felt just like winning a Super Bowl, but his role was different. "I can't take much credit," said Gibbs. "My job is to pray and stay out of the way."[7]

Eighteen months before this Valentine's Day success, the Gibbs-Jarrett team didn't even exist. In seven fateful days in July, 1991, Joe Gibbs linked up with a creative risk-taker and marketing man named Norm Miller. Miller, down in the pit that day cheering, jumping, and praying right next to Coach Gibbs, is the chairman of the board of Interstate Batteries, lead sponsor of the car. What kind of a man is Norm Miller that Joe Gibbs would want to have a close sponsorship association with him? And what would make a recognized business executive turn to prayer in the middle of a race? The answer is someone with a rock-solid value system, whose ethics are firm and consistent on the job and at the racetrack.

RIDE THE PIPELINE

Ironically, Norm Miller's life dream is not to race a stock car; it's to "ride the Pipeline." The Pipeline is the name given to a well-known surfing spot on the north shore of Oahu, Hawaii, made famous because the waves are so large that when they break they form a perfect curl or tube, making this the greatest surfing challenge in the world. The ultimate in surfing is to shoot the curl at the Pipeline when the waves are up. The curl is the hollow of the wave, the sweet spot just inside the base of the wave's crest where a surfer dreams of having the perfect ride—like those pictures on "Wide World of Sports." The wave curls above you, obscuring the sun and propelling the surfboard forward.

From the shoreline the surfer, small and fragile, is dwarfed by the towering twenty-foot wave. He stands skillfully on his tiny board, totally unprotected, exposed to all the power of the water, taking some of the greatest forces of nature head-on. Engulfed by the spray of the wave, the surfer disappears, only to reappear out of the mist, still upright on his board, staying with it until the wave laps the shore. He has survived the greatest challenge and risk in surfing; he has ridden the Pipeline.

What makes a man want to be this kind of risk-taker in life? Certainly Norm Miller has many reasons not to take risks. A lot is at stake for the chairman of the board of the Number 1 replacement battery company in America. Shortly after graduating from North Texas State University in 1962, Norm joined his father's distributorship in Memphis as a salesman and a route truck manager for Interstate Battery System of America, Inc. In 1965 Norm moved to Interstate's national headquarters in Dallas. Founded in 1961 by John Searcy, the aim of Interstate was to develop a national sales and distribution system of replacement batteries through privately owned and operated distributorships. The market for which they aimed was specifically defined trade areas based on vehicle registrations. The emphasis of the program was to offer the traditional retail trade, primarily service stations, garages, and car dealers, a premium quality battery on a consignment basis backed by a liberal on-the-spot warranty. This approach is the basis for Interstate's business to this day and is the key to their success.

In 1965, when Norm joined John Searcy, his mentor, at the home office, thirty-five distributorships were selling about a quarter-of-a-million batteries a year. During 1969, the year Tommy Miller, Norm's younger brother, joined Interstate, sales had increased to more than one-half million. Through the addition of more field salesmen in 1970, expansion continued, and in 1976 for the first time Interstate sold a million batteries. By 1978, that figure had doubled. In 1978 John Searcy retired and sold controlling interest in the company to Norm.

Under Norm's leadership, sales continued their upward march. In 1980 Interstate's sales reached three million, and in 1982 sales moved up a notch to four million. At the beginning of 1993 there were 350 distributors and 205,000 dealers across all of the United States and Canada. Unit battery sales have broken record after record, reaching more than 8.7 million batteries sold in 1992. Interstate Batteries outsells everybody in the battery replacement field, including GM's Delco and Sears' highly publicized Diehard. In terms of sales, Interstate Batteries are the best in the field.

In 1983 Norm Miller joined with one of his old buddies, Tom McRae, to sponsor the Great American Race, a coast-to-coast antique car race featuring some of the most fabulous cars ever—cars such as the 1907 Thomas Flyer, winner of the original Great Race run from New York to Paris in 1908; a 1909 Mercedes four-cylinder that could do 127 miles an hour; and Bonnie and Clyde's death car, bullet holes and all.

In 1990, Norm relinquished the title of President to Tommy, his brother, in order to spend more time focusing on other strategies and issues facing the company. Their combined leadership continues to lift the company to higher levels than previously achieved.

Even though Norm Miller has many reasons not to take risks, he has been a risk-taker all his life, and there was a time when it nearly killed him. Literally. To know Norm Miller's vision and ethics today, you have to look at that nearly deadly past.

WINE, WOMEN, AND SONG

The Miller boys grew up on Galveston Island just off the Texas coast in the Gulf of Mexico. Galveston was a bustling, bawdy war town and port with a reputation for wine, women, song, and gambling (most of which was illegal) that could trace its heritage all the way back to Jean Lafitte, the pirate who made his home there in the 1800s. Their father had opened a Gulf Oil Service Station, and he enjoyed the loud, sometimes rowdy tone of the town. Every Saturday afternoon about two o'clock, Norm's dad would set up a bar in the back room of the station. Joined by some of his regular customers, all the senior Miller wanted to do was have a little fun, fun which usually lasted until around eight in the evening when the other men would carry him home and put him to bed.

Like so many sons, Norm followed his father's footsteps and began drinking when he was fourteen and in junior high school. His major game plan, learned from his father, was fun and partying which he pursued through high school and college. Upon graduation from college, he added a few new goals: business success, the ideal wife and family, and a dream home. Here was Norm's Pipeline: good job, impressive title, good money, pretty wife, pretty kids (one of each gender), and the opportunity to party and travel.

By 1974, at age thirty-five, Norm had reached all his goals ahead of time. But there was one problem: there was no payoff, no fulfillment. He was left asking himself, *Is this all there is?* Drinking had become a major issue in his life, and his wife had decided to leave him. He started to collect DWI (driving while intoxicated) tickets and woke up one morning terrified after driving drunk because he knew he had planned not to get drunk the night before, didn't even want to get drunk, but he couldn't stop himself. Lying on his bed, Norm Miller realized that, like his father before him, he was an alcoholic who had lost control of his life. He was like a surfer who had lost his ride on the Pipeline. The wave had crashed down on him, and he was churning through the water, surfboard gone, the force and power of it all driving him toward shore and threatening to push him underwater, gasping for air.

Rising star of Interstate Battery and all his life dreams coming true; yet those dreams were slipping through his fingers at the same time. In panic and desperation he cried out, "God, help me, I can't handle it." In that very moment, God, in His mercy, heard his plea and took his alcoholism from him. Although this rarely occurs, it is exactly what happened to Norm Miller.

The next step was to try Alcoholics Anonymous for a few weeks. He read some of their materials and was reinforced in his thinking by their emphasis on a Supreme Being. Some in the program told him, off the record, that only those who became "Christians" gained freedom from alcohol on a long-term basis. That idea had no appeal for Norm Miller. Church was the last thing he needed. The Bible was a collection of illogical nonsense as far as he was concerned, and he had better things to do with himself than get involved with something like that.

THE BIBLE?

About that time Tom Crocker, a friend of Norm's, started telling him what the Bible had to say about life and how to live it. Norm quickly cut him off with a challenge he thought Tom could not meet. He said, "If you can show me how I can buy the Bible as the truth, logically with my brain, then I'll pay attention to what it has to say. Otherwise, as far as I'm concerned, it's just another old book, a bunch of people's outdated philosophies or whatever, and I don't need it." In Norm's mind that ended that. But his friend met him head on and showed up with some books that documented the validity of the claim that the Bible is God's truth. Norm was overwhelmed by the objective evidence concerning the Bible from three major sources: archaeological discoveries, manuscript authenticity, and the fulfillment of Old Testament prophecy hundreds of years later in the New Testament. One of the key books that changed Norm's thinking was Josh McDowell's work *Evidence That Demands a Verdict.*

What seemed complicated soon began to make sense. He learned that the Bible is broken down into two major divisions, the Old Testament or Old Covenant and the New Testament or New Covenant. A covenant is an agreement between two people that determines how they will relate to one another and live together. The covenants in the Bible were made by God at His initiative to define how men and women can live together in harmony with Him so He can bring love, hope, and peace into our lives. Actually, there are more than two covenants in the Bible, but the primary focus is on the Old and the New. The Old Covenant promised the coming of Jesus, God's Son, who would bring God's love to mankind; the New Covenant fulfills that promise and makes His love available to all who will trust in Jesus as God's Son. Jesus is presented as the one who can set us free from our own self-destructive tendencies and bring us deliverance and peace with God. These two covenants are broken down into smaller segments called books, and there are sixty-six books in the Bible.

Many of the books have names which were foreign to Norm, but when he—like any reader—got into them he discovered that they deal with the same emotional and relational struggles he faced.

This is the reason why the Bible has endured across centuries and cultures. Its timeless message cuts across every time warp and every cultural wall because it brings healing for the most desperate pain men and women face. Norm Miller discovered this truth when he began to explore the Bible as a credible message to a man who stood on the brink of wipeout even though all his dreams had come true.

Because the evidence convinced him that the Bible is the Word of God, Norm began to read it. As he read, he discovered statements which motivated him to look further. When he read that famous statement, "Seek and ye shall find" (Matthew 7:7), he told God, "If You are for real, I am a seeker." Since the promise said "shall" and not "may," Norm was confident he would find the truth. He read the claim of Jesus, "I am the way, the truth, and the life" (John 14:6), and he was searching for the way that would bring him the truth resulting in life. He longed for freedom, and he read that the truth would set him free.[8] He realized that his life-style did not please God, that he owed God for the way he was living, but that he could not pay God for what he had done to his family and himself. He grasped the fact that Jesus had died to pay what he owed God and that he needed to humble himself, change his mind about the way he thought about Jesus, and trust Him alone for forgiveness and the ability to live life God's way. Now he had to make a decision.

Norm and his wife, Anne, had been invited to a five-week home discussion forum sponsored by Search Ministries and hosted by their friends, Tom and Linda Crocker, and then to a Bible study that followed the forum. Although they could not attend the five-week discussion, they were able to participate in the Bible study. Here Norm learned some of the key passages that would soon influence his life and control his values. He already knew he was unable to live effectively on his own and that God had delivered him from alcohol that desperate morning when he called on Him for help. But as he participated in the Bible study, he questioned the claim that Jesus is God and the Son of God. However, when others in the study showed him the biblical evidence for this claim, he realized he needed to make a decision about Christ. For two hours one night following the Bible study he sat and talked with the leader, Miles Lorenzen, about his questions.

"I knew I was a sinner," Norm recalls. "I believed in God and in Jesus as His Son. I knew Jesus died on the cross for me to pay for my disobedience. Finally, at midnight, I decided to receive Him in my heart as my Lord and Savior." At that point, Norm told God he knew he had disobeyed Him, that Jesus had died to pay for that disobedience, and then he told Jesus he wanted to trust Him not only for eternal life but for the power to live life here and now.

Driving home that night he asked himself, *Norm, what have you done?* "I felt like I was in an Alfred Hitchcock movie and everything was unreal. So, when I got home at midnight or later, I went to my family room to be by myself, opened the Bible, and asked God to confirm the commitment I had made. And, after some time reading the Bible, praying a while longer, and a restless night's sleep, I woke up convinced that I had done the right thing. From that early morning moment in 1974 on, I have never doubted my decision to trust Christ."

FROM FEAR TO LOVE

While he was searching for understanding in that Bible study before he committed himself to Christ, he came across a statement that spoke of the fruit of the Spirit,[9] i.e., what God's Spirit would do in his life if he would trust in Jesus. He was attracted to the promise of love, joy, and peace because he had never known any of these previously, especially love. The driving force in Norm's life before this had been fear, the fear of failure, the fear of falling behind his peers. He did not love. He only cared for people, even his family, based on how they treated or served him. But this changed following his decision to trust Christ.

Along with the release from fear to love, there was another change that came in Norm after receiving Christ. He determined to leave the results of his work and plans up to God. Of course, he still plans and strives for excellence as God wants him to, but making money no longer controls his life. Once money was a god in his life. Today it is not. Instead, this new love has focused him on the true God and His values. For Norm Miller, coming in first has taken on a whole new meaning. He now lives beyond the bottom line at the place of trust where his faith defines what coming in first means. Norm comes in first when he takes the risk of trusting God and strives to obey Him in every decision even when it doesn't seem to make hard-headed business sense. He now seeks to choose for God instead of self.

What kind of convictions bring about this sort of transformation? Norm had to learn a whole new set of principles from the Bible concerning the amassing and management of money. These principles demand radically new values and commitments that completely change our attitudes toward possessions. They redefine what coming in first is. Let's look at these truths and then see how Norm applies them to his business life.

FIRST THINGS FIRST

One of the things Norm learned was how to make a good investment. When he read these words of Jesus he realized how foolishly he had invested his life for the first thirty-five years: "Do not store up for yourselves treasures on earth, where moth and rust destroy, and where thieves break in and steal. But store up for yourselves treasures in heaven, where moth and rust do not destroy, and where thieves do not break in. For where your treasure is, there your heart will be also"(Matthew 6:19–21). Who would ever invest in a warehouse full of rusted out auto parts or moth eaten suits, or put thousands of dollars into property located in a high crime area? No one in his right mind. Yet, this is what Norm was doing when he made wealth his security.

Norm saw this once he trusted Christ, so he acted by doing what Jesus called for when He said, "But seek first his [God's] kingdom and his righteousness, and all these things [material needs] will be added to you" (Matthew 6:33) . Norm determined to make this choice: to put God's interests first in every aspect of his business and to do things the right way, God's way, whether or not it made sense according to the management consultants or the human resources people or the financial advisers. *God first* and *God's way the only way* became Norm's measuring standard of all he does. He seeks to put God's interests first and tries to trust God to take care of his interests.

This is not to say that Norm is on target 100 percent of the time. No one whose family has passed through nearly fifteen years of alcoholism can escape unscathed, and Norm hasn't. There have been hard and demanding days in the years since he made his decision to live Christ's way, and Norm has not always lived up to his own ideals. But his commitment has remained unchanged, and he continues to strive to come in first in a new way, not by pleasure-driven partying and fear-driven financial accumulation, but by releasing all he owns to honor God however he can. Though Norm has not yet surfed Oahu's Pipeline, he rides a different kind of exhilarating Pipeline, one that propels him to risk all by obeying God to the best of his desire and intention. Here is what it means to please God from Norm Miller's perspective: to risk all if this is what it takes to obey God.

COMMITTED TO LOVE

Once Norm committed himself to put God first, he discovered what this required: to love God and neighbor.[10] "To love God is to obey Him, and to love my neighbors is to do everything I can to meet their needs," he says. For Norm, this meant that God owned everything he once called his own, and he desired that all he did twenty-four hours a day until his death should be 100 percent pleasing to Him: "As I see it, if a guy is 100 percent sold out to selling insurance, every living human being he meets is a prospect. [Similarly] I'm supposed to love God and others, so I just try to stay attuned to God's mandate that I'm supposed to either be leading people to Christ or helping them grow in Christ. Leading, pointing, and growing—that's what life is all about as far as I'm concerned.

"If God allows me a platform, that platform becomes an asset, not just for me, but for the owner, God. I'm going to have to stand before God one day and be appraised as to how I used my asset. If you want to please God, you can't run a business and behave in a way that's not loving and kind. Some say the business world is dog-eat-dog, and you can't make it if you don't play the game that way.... God's mandate is more important than business."

After reading Luke 12:4–5, Christ's warning to fear our future Judge instead of people who can hurt us only temporarily, Norm concluded his actions must always please God before pleasing people: "So, if profit conflicts with obeying God, I try to obey God. I only want whatever God wants me to have."

FOCUSED ON FAITH

When Norm first became a believer and started reading the Scriptures, he discovered that the only way to please God is to trust Him no matter what. "Without faith it is impossible to please God" (Hebrews 11:6). This became the new Pipeline for Norm, the new risk he would take. Trusting God became the surf he would now ride, the new rising, towering, wall of water forming the curl of his new Pipeline. Now he takes risks out of gratitude for his freedom from fear and the newfound love which fills his heart. The point of this became very specific when he read further in the Bible that he should trust God for every life need. This had two implications for his life-style: first, that he should never cheat to get money in any way, whether in dealing with investors, employees, suppliers, customers, or on income taxes; second, that he should invest in God's purposes generously and with a cheerful heart.

When it came to income taxes, Norm decided to be totally honest because he only wanted to accept the money God wanted him to have. Since all money is God's money, and He can give whatever He wants, Norm determined never to gain a dime by using methods that are contrary to God's ways. He soon faced a test of that decision.

Shortly after he made that commitment, Norm decided to take a vacation on the Snake River in Idaho. He and his family would float down the river and, since he had a customer in Twin Falls, he decided to stop and conduct a little business. Because he was going to visit with a customer and take him out to dinner, he chose to charge the airfare for the entire trip to the company and save himself $410, a large sum to him in those days. He stopped in Twin Falls for just one day, saw his customer, went to the warehouse, talked about business, and took him out to dinner. But after he got back from his vacation he started to fret over the legality of what he had done. He went to his boss and spoke to him about his concerns. His boss told him to talk to the accounting firm that served the company, and they said it all came down to the intent of the trip. If he were going specifically to see the customer, it was appropriate to charge the bill to Interstate even if he took a vacation for a few days. However, if doing business was incidental to a vacation trip, all he could write off was one day's car rental and food plus the cost of a hotel for one night. Norm now faced a dilemma since he had already submitted the cost as a company expense and he did need the $410. But he chose to write a check for the full amount to Interstate because he only wanted the money God intended him to have. He would not take it by illegal means, even if his action were never discovered.

Norm has been called to write other checks, checks to those whom God has directed him to help. In the Bible he read if someone asks you for help you should give it to him if you are convinced it's good stewardship.[11] He also discovered the verses we have seen earlier exhorting us to lay up treasure in heaven. Norm added to these other portions containing the stewardship parables that showed him he does not own anything in the total sense of the word "ownership." Although Norm is the Chairman of the Board and the majority owner, he views himself as the branch manager of Interstate. In his mind, God is the owner of the company who has informed him through the Bible to keep what he needs for his family and the development of the company and use the rest for ministry to promote and grow God's business of caring for the spiritually and physically hurting. For this reason, Norm hired Jim Cote to be a chaplain for Interstate to minister to the employees and to help in the giving ministry.

When Norm and Jim sit down to determine how to invest in God's interests, they face both a tension and a dilemma because God has left so much up to all of us in relation to money. Even though He has provided us with specific directions about giving, He has also given us a great deal of freedom in determining how much we need for ourselves and how much we should give to others. For this reason, they pray much about the difficult decisions concerning how contributions should be managed. By nature, these decisions are subjective and uncertain, and Norm seeks to bring clarity to what they are doing by moving cautiously and by prayerfully establishing specific criteria from which they seldom vary.

For example, for some time Norm has had a desire to build a racetrack which would feature Interstate Batteries' name as a means of creating visibility and image in order to increase company sales. The plan was to offer memberships to those who owned cars they wanted to race. Several years ago, after praying, he determined to approach three investors who shared his convictions and his interests and partner with any one of them in this project. They had to have the same commitments and values he had before he would approach them. He determined that if none of the three men chose to participate, he would look no further and take this as an indication that God was not in it and he should not do it.

The first man he called did not know Norm, didn't like the idea, and turned it down over the phone. Norm knew the second man, but, likewise, he was not interested and turned down the opportunity. The third man, however, was interested enough to meet with Norm three times before deciding he too did not want to invest. So Norm's dream of a racetrack never came into being. However, within a year after that, oil prices fell from $30 a barrel to $10 instead of the $40 they were supposed to reach, and land prices fell 30 to 40 percent, so all those who could have participated were busily scrambling to survive. The project was doomed to failure, although Norm didn't know that at the time he established the conditions governing his decision. His conditions, determined through prayer, kept him from a disastrous investment.

But it is exceedingly dangerous to conclude that prayer is some sort of magic guardrail that will keep all who practice it on the highway to prosperity. For every positive example like this one, there are scores of negative experiences in which those involved may have been equally cautious, equally prayerful, and equally dedicated, but who found the investors at exactly the wrong time and lost everything. I present this as an example of how one man makes decisions, not as a ruling standard for all. Even though Norm prays about each of his investments, not all of them turn out to be profitable. He has also surrounded himself with advisers who help him frame his conditions and seek to determine his timing in order to discipline his entrepreneurial risk taking. Some of it has to do with the way God has made him, His divine design affirmed over a lifetime of business and experience. Behind Norm's subjectivity there is a high level of wisdom harvested from years of work in business. All of this comes together in the decision-making process as Norm considers the handling of God's money.

FACE THE *MUSIG*

When it comes to giving money, i.e., investing in God's interests, Norm wants to get as large a return as possible. In order to create objectivity in the giving process, he and Jim Cote developed a grid around the acronym *MUSIG*, in which each letter stands for a measuring standard used to determine whether or not they should give to a particular project.

"M" stands for multiplication. If the most important response in life is to love God and others, the most loving act in life is to provide others with the opportunity to know God through the Lord Jesus Christ. This puts the multiplication of the good news concerning new life through belief in Jesus Christ as God's Son number one on the list of spiritual investments. To pass the first test on the Miller grid, the request must be one that multiplies the number of people who will hear this good news as well as the number of people who will be trained to carry it to others. It is not just enough to tell others about Jesus for Norm to invest in a ministry; there must also be the intention to reproduce reproducers, to build in the lives of the new believers so they can take the message to still others who have not yet responded. An example of this is the university ministry of Campus Crusade in which many transferable concepts are used to train both old and new believers in reaching others.

"U" stands for urgency. A strategy for multiplication is number one, but the urgency of the opportunity is also very significant. For example, the intense spiritual responsiveness in the former Soviet Union pushes it to the very top of the list. But can it pass the second test, the test of urgency? How much time do we have in the Confederation of Independent States in comparison to other parts of the world? Is there a part of the world that may not represent as great an opportunity but, due to war or economic collapse or spiritual opposition, may be closing down soon? If so, this situation will receive attention. However, since no one is certain how long the door will be open in Russia and the surrounding countries, situations there present both multiplication and urgency, so they would tend to stay at the top of the list.

"S" stands for scope. Some situations offer a very focused opportunity for urgent multiplication, whereas others present a larger scope. For Norm Miller, a broader scope can represent a better spiritual investment for the long term. This will not be true for everyone, of course. Some have specific interests due to their cultural background, personal pilgrimage, or some other influence that calls their attention to a particular need. The point is that everyone must take the scope of an opportunity into consideration when making decisions on spiritual investing opportunities.

Scope speaks of how large a potential for impact the venture has. A ministry that is focused in a specific individual toward a particular geographical setting may have great multiplication potential, but its scope could be quite narrow. Since there's only one individual and the ministry is unique to him, the skills cannot easily be reproduced. If this person has no management ability, and no one is building him up or holding him accountable, the scope of his ministry will be limited, and this makes it a bad investment for Miller. On the other hand, the Jesus film teams employ transferable processes and have a much broader impact than any single individual could ever have. This makes them a good investment in Norm's mind.

"I" stands for impact. Impact deals with the issue of timing and efficiency, and with the management of the organization involved. How long will the money be tied up? How rapidly will it get to the action point? How much of it will be used for administrative overhead compared to how much of it will get to the front lines? How efficient is the organization overall in managing its vision and its funds? What are they planning to do in the next year that shows them to be worthy recipients of the money?

Impact questions such as these must be asked before the money is released, not only because this is good stewardship but because giving must be done without intent to control. One of the key thoughts contained in the biblical command that those with the gift of giving should give generously[13] is that they give without attempting to control or to buy influence. It is not the giver's responsibility to co-opt the vision of an organization but to help accomplish it. If the giver cannot release the money without concern, the funds should be directed to another opportunity. However, the giver has a perfect right and responsibility to establish accountability standards in accordance with the stated purpose of the organization. To expect and receive reports of the impact of the gift is both a courtesy on the part of the receiving organization and an encouragement to the donor.

"G" stands for growth. Growth relates primarily to the ministry venture's potential to be duplicated. If it is tied primarily to one event or a specific personality, then it may not be easily reproducible, which could mean that growth will be slow or impossible. Norm and Jim like to choose ministries that not only fulfill their immediate objectives as presented, but also those that can successfully be duplicated in other situations. A secular example of growth is the McDonald's chain which has been established in every setting imaginable, from urban centers to suburban shopping strips to interstate highway exits to small towns. A spiritual example of growth is the *Jesus* film teams of Campus Crusade mentioned above. Such

teams operate all over the world in even more settings than McDonald's. Not only can these teams successfully adapt to every culture and condition in the world; they can be made up of people of all ages and both genders. With a relatively small amount of training, people from college students to senior citizens can effectively use this medium. This ministry can grow, which makes it a good investment.

Growth also relates to the internal organizational integrity of the ministry making the appeal. Do they have the administrative manpower and systems necessary to sustain growth? Are their projections accurate? Is it reasonable to expect them to fulfill their goals? All these factors affect growth.

Finally, growth looks at the historical timing or potential of the ministry. Are they in a field that has diminished, or is the field increasing in its ministry opportunity? For example, one military ministry Norm has been supporting will be terminated in the next year when the Air Force base it serves is closed. Obviously, this ministry does not have much growth potential and will gain no future support.

Beyond all of these guidelines, one of the major spiritual investments Norm makes is to theological education, because this is where much of the leadership for front line organizations is developed. The understanding of biblical truth is so foundational to all that is attempted and accomplished that Norm believes this should receive particular attention, since the foundation determines how well the effort fares.

GO WITH THE *FLO*

Along with his desire to invest financially in God's interests, Norm has also determined that he should give of himself through his time and talents to help spiritually focused organizations accomplish their aims. He also wants to find and involve others who share his interests by providing them with ministry opportunities here in the U.S. and elsewhere in the world to travel on short-term outreach missions. To do this, Norm and Anne have established a separate ministry and have hired a full-time director, Tom Greene, to head up what they have named FLO, Front Line Outreach.

As Norm states in the information he has developed concerning this project, "The purpose of FLO is to help Christians draw 'closer to God' through experiencing the wonderful fulfillment of being used by Him in hands on, front line evangelism and discipleship! FLO targets specific ministry opportunities for believers who want to personally participate, one-on-one, in fulfilling the great commission on short term mission trips here in the United States as well as throughout the world. This is accomplished by teaming up with existing missionary groups that are clearly being led and blessed by the Spirit of God."

Norm seeks to interest people in local (Dallas), national, and international opportunities through a series of selected organizations. For him, this is simply an extension of what it means to love God and others and ride the Pipeline of faith.

COMING IN FIRST

Valentine's Day, 1993. Daytona Beach, Florida. A great day for the running of the Daytona 500.

More than 100,000 rise from their seats to cheer Dale Earnhardt and Jarrett, side-by-side, coming out of the last turn. Heading for the flag, the two cars roar and the fans shout. Meanwhile, down in the pits, the Garrett team is cheering, jumping up-and-down, and praying all at the same time. In the TV announcers' booth, one man exhorts his son: "Come on, Dale, win! Come on, Dale, come in first!"

On this team, the team that was coming in first, was Norm Miller, a man who has sought to come in first all of his life. He used to come in first by partying and working to make money. But, in those days, he was coming in last, driven by fear, a selfish and unloving man. Norm still wants to come in first, but now he strives to come in first God's way through love for Him and others and a faith that seeks to obey God no matter what it might cost or how foolish it might seem. Now Norm sees himself as a branch manager of God's business stationed at Interstate Batteries, working to invest God's resources in ways that please Him, knowing full well that someday he will give an accounting of his management to Him.

Today, Norm Miller seeks to ride the Pipeline God's way, to be a risk-taker, to settle on his surfboard at the foot of a surging wall of water and negotiate his way to the shore by loving and trusting God. Convince him that trusting and obeying God demands a specific step, and he will take it. He will certainly attempt to be wise in all he does. He will pray and draw upon his thirty years of business experience as well as the cadre of close advisers, both family and friends, who have much at stake in whatever happens. But if he believes God wants it done, he will strive to do it. No one can do this all the time, but Norm makes the best effort he can.

Norm Miller lives for coming in first by striving to put God's interests above all others and by doing his best to manage his business God's way, ethically, lovingly, and generously. This is the only way to come in first. And this is what it means for Norm Miller to go beyond the bottom line to the place where faith and business meet.

CHAPTER EIGHT

HOT DOG WRAPPER OR STALLION?

R obert Young was a dapper, pint-sized Texan with an ambition as big as the Lone Star State itself. Ron Chernow, writing in *The House of Morgan,* describes how Young left Texas for New York to become one of the greatest railroad magnates of this century.[1] At one point, he controlled six railroads and was the chairman of the Chesapeake and Ohio, the famous C&O. His enormous wealth enabled him to own a Tudor mansion in Newport, a Spanish villa in Palm Beach, and a sumptuous apartment in Manhattan's Waldorf Towers. The great focus of his life and ambition, however, was the House of Morgan, the famous banking empire established by J. Pierpont Morgan and carried on by his son, Jack. In an early confrontation with Morgan interests, Young was defeated, and he never forgot or forgave that loss.

BRING DOWN THE HOUSE

By the early 1950s, Young's driving ambition was to bring down the House of Morgan. His first attempt occurred when he testified against them in a suit brought by the Justice Department. However, he was such a vitriolic witness that Judge Harold Medina refused to shake his extended hand following his testimony. His second attempt, an effort to take over the New York Central, proved to be more successful. By late 1953, he had amassed one million shares, 21 percent of New York Central stock. Despite that, the directors wouldn't even give him a seat on the board, so he launched a proxy fight which he eventually won. By winning, Young not only unseated the Morgans but also broke the last vestiges of Vanderbilt control over the system. The Commodore himself had established the New York Central, and it was once wholly owned by the Vanderbilt family. What a win! A little man from the hinterlands of Texas defeated the biggest boys in the Eastern establishment.

Unfortunately, it turned out to be a pyrrhic victory. With the construction of the interstate highway system and the development of the jet airplane, the railroad was being outmoded, and the New York Central was bankrupt. Robert Young's blazing ambition blinded him to the emerging realities of modern transportation. He had used all his resources, as well as the resources of others, to gain control of a dinosaur. Once he realized this, he attempted to create a merger with the Pennsylvania Railroad, but this was a futile effort. Depression surrounded Young like a deep shroud. A friend, Edward Stettinius, once found him alone in his Newport library staring absently into space, a gun on his desk. On January 25, 1958, in the billiard room of his Palm Beach mansion, Robert Young took a gun and shot himself to death.

Robert Young, dapper, pint-sized Texan, railroad magnate, little David against the giant House of Morgan, possessed by the driving force of great dreams, was drawn to his death by the burning flame of his own ambition. Ambition, the fuel that energizes all human achievement, ignited into an explosive fire that consumed his life and turned it into the charred ruins of an ego flameout.

BLINDING AMBITION

Haman, adviser to the ancient Persian king, Ahasuerus, lived long before Robert Young, but died of the same disease. Haman longed to occupy the top position in the kingdom next to the king himself, but he had one barrier: the Jews. He came to despise the Jews, especially one who became the focus of his drivenness, Mordecai, uncle of the queen, Esther. Unfortunately, Haman did not know of this relationship. One night when Ahasuerus could not sleep, he asked one of his attendants to read the royal records to him. Through this reading, the king discovered that Mordecai had once brought warning of an attempt on his life, and Ahasuerus became concerned that this aged Jew be rewarded appropriately. But what could he do?

The next morning, when Haman arrived at the court, Ahasuerus asked him, "What should the king do to reward the man he most wants to honor in the kingdom?" Haman, assuming he was that man, came up with the greatest public display of honor he could conceive: such a man should be attired in the king's best garment, ride the king's best steed, and be led through the streets to the accolades of the crowds. What a shock it was for Haman to discover that Mordecai was the man to be honored and he was the man who would lead him through the streets crying out his greatness. Selfish ambition has a way of turning on its admirers.

Unfortunately, self-focused ambition can also blind those who seek to accomplish its destructive demands. Infuriated by the turn of events, Haman decided to destroy Mordecai by wiping out every Jew in the kingdom. In anticipation of this action, he built a gallows on which he planned to hang his enemy. At this point Haman's unawareness of Esther's ancestry became a problem for him. Esther made her race known to the king, and the Jews were given permission to defend themselves. The result? Irony of all irony, at the direct command of the king Haman and his family were hung on the very gallows he planned for Mordecai.

Haman, would-be power in the kingdom of Ahasuerus, top adviser to the king, rising star of Persia, was driven to his death by the arrogance of his ambition. Ambition, the fuel that energizes all human achievement, turned on him, blinded him, and choked his very life out of him in a public display of shame.

AMBITION: FRUITFUL FORCE OR FATEFUL FORCE?

In the workplace, ambition is a powerful force that sometimes grips us with drivenness. It leaves us with a frustrating sense of failure when these dreams turn out to be mere mirages in our imaginations. What can we do with the energy of ambition? Is ambition a fruitful force, energizing and freeing us to fulfill ourselves and become what we are designed to be from the hand of God? Or is ambition a fateful force, driving us to selfishness and personal destruction as we push others aside to achieve our aims at their expense?

We answer this question when we realize that ambition demands a choice, a choice between selfish ambition and servant ambition. Selfish ambition looks out for itself, seeks its own ends, exalts its own position, and can only be satisfied by one thing: more. The selfishly ambitious become self-made throwaway people, a kind of human hot dog wrapper.

Service ambition, on the other hand, looks out for others and delights in meeting those needs as an act of honor to the Lord. It seeks the Lord's ends, exalts Him, and works only to satisfy Him with all of its energy. Such servants receive few accolades but are assured in their actions; they are pictured by the mighty stallion. So we must understand that ambition demands a choice, a choice that will make us either a hot dog wrapper or a stallion.

Like most external and internal resources we have, ambition is not inherently evil. How we regard it and what we do with it can lead to good. It's similar to resources such as money, power, influence, and position. *Money* cannot be our master, but we must have it to live and serve God. Remember, the apostle Paul; did not say "Money is a root of all evil" but rather "the love of money is a root of all kinds of evil" (1 Timothy 6:10). When money masters us, greed dominates us, and that is the sin.

Power is equally imperative if we are to be effective, as we can see through such biblical figures as Joseph and Daniel who were put into secular power positions in order to accomplish God's ends. Their authority allowed them to accomplish much good. Anyone familiar with today's business scene knows power is essential for effectiveness.

This is also true for *influence*, and we see this biblically when Paul sent men such as Timothy and Titus to act in his place. Paul delegated his authority so they could exercise the influence necessary to bring about the changes for the health of his enterprise. The essence of management and business leadership is the appropriate exercise of influence, also a force needed for the health of the enterprise.

Finally, there is *position*. Paul did not hesitate to use his position as a Roman citizen to protect himself from persecution and death in order to accomplish his goals in the ancient world. Men and women in the right position, who use the prerogatives position gives, can have an immense influence on the moral/ethical direction of a corporation.

Money, power, influence, and position are often regarded negatively in the Christian community, sometimes with good reason. Yet, all of these can accomplish very good ends. In fact, no good end can be accomplished apart from these elements, and ambition is essential for all of these. Ambition is the fuel, the energy, that moves us forward in life to attain the money, power, influence, and position that enable us to be effective for Christ.

TWIN KILLERS

Writing in the New Testament, James, the half-brother of Jesus, addresses leaders with an important question, a character question. He asks, "Who is wise and understanding among you?" (James 3:13) i.e., who has the practical insight and essential knowledge to live life in a mature way? In answering his own question, James warns us against a set of twin killers that destroy character and ethics in leaders, the flaws of bitter jealousy and selfish ambition. On your job, as either a worker or manager, you must watch out for those twins, for they can destroy your ethics and turn you into useless hot dog wrappers.

First, let's consider jealousy. Bitter jealousy acts like acid in the emotional system, eating away at our souls, burning holes in our perspective, creating anger and hatred in our spirits. A spirit of bitterness arises and blinds us to realities about ourselves and those around us, making us gods in our own little egocentric universes while keeping us from seeing how small we actually are. Tragically, the bigness we often seek for ourselves comes because of the smallness we innately sense in ourselves. No one who is motivated by bitter jealousy can have either the wisdom or the understanding needed to lead others.

Selfish ambition is the driving need to show our superiority over others, to achieve more than anyone else, to prove that we are better than the rest. The heart of selfish ambition is drivenness, a throbbing, pulsating inner compulsion to beat others to the top and to stay there the longest no matter what. Often such driven people are nice people, decent people, Christian people, who achieve much good. Gordon MacDonald describes them well in his book, *Ordering Your Private World.*

> There are lots of driven people doing very good things. Driven people are not necessarily bad folk, although the consequences of their drivenness may produce unfortunate results. In fact, driven people often make great contributions. They start organizations; they provide jobs and opportunities; they are often very bright and offer ways and means of doing things that benefit many other people. But nevertheless they are driven, and one worries about their ability to sustain the pace without danger to themselves.[2]

Over a period of time the good that driven people do turns out to be a thin skin of selflessness. Underneath exists a heart of selfishness, and eventually the skin wears away to revel the heart that pounds with ambition and that eventually wounds others. If you want to know whether a man is selfishly ambitious, look at his wife and his children. This will tell you much of what you need to know. The unselfish man desires to meet their needs, not just by providing food and clothes but offering comfort and his very presence; he will not consume his spare time with golf, business contacts and personal development. The great sign of drivenness is stress,[3] stress in the man and stress in his family. Since winning is more important than anything else for most driven people, relationships, even the most precious, are not high enough on their scale of significance to make driven men and women give the same energy to them that they give to becoming Number 1.

In fact, selfishly ambitious executives create a stressful home environment for their children that has a severely harmful impact on children:

> When emotionally distant executives who are away from home most of the time impose on their children their own stringent work ethic and sky-high expectations, the result is a stressful home environment that is harmful to the children. Upwardly mobile executives, especially when they are men, tend not to be involved in their children's day-to-day lives and are most likely to pay attention to their children's successes and failures.[4]

Typically, they attract those children who are like them and alienate those who are different. "Executives cherishing high aspirations for their children predictably end up closest to the children—often firstborn—who fulfill these aspirations and most distant (or even estranged) from those children who reject the sacred value placed on achievement."[5] One statistic says it all. "Children of executives were more than twice as likely as children of non-executives to receive treatment for psychiatric problems or drug abuse."[6]

In its essence, selfish ambition is the driving need to be Number 1 no matter what it costs. It is the drive to mastery, the inner demand for it, the willingness to pursue it with great energy, the readiness to push other people hard to grasp it, and the hunger for the rewards it brings. This ambition also cannot stand to be without such mastery. Not to have mastery is to fail, and this, the greatest failure possible to those who must be Number 1, brings immense pain, the worst pain they can ever experience. They will do virtually anything to avoid such pain.[7]

DUAL PAIN

One of the inherent marks of selfish ambition is deceit. This grows out of the way the concept of deceit developed in James's day when it described politicians who promised to serve for the public good but who actually served themselves for their private good. This deceit expresses itself in a number of ways.

First, selfish ambition deceives its victims so they are utterly unable to see what is obvious to so many around them: they are more interested in themselves and their own interests than in anything or anyone else. Thus selfish ambition deceives its possessor into thinking he is doing good, building a company, helping society, making a difference, when he is in fact headed for disorder and every kind of evil, as James says later in his analysis.

Second, selfish ambition deceives its victims by telling them how humble it is, how helpful it is, how much it cares for them while inside itself it focuses on its own superiority and how great it is in contrast to others.

James tells us this dual deception leads the selfishly ambitious to bear their inevitable fruit: disorder and every evil thing.[8]

COMPANY CHAOS

A company led by selfish ambition is a company in chaos, a company full of ethical weeds. The people at the top will be focused on their own fortunes with the dollar ruling as king and the bottom line being the only line that counts. If selfish ambition runs manufacturing, shoddy material will be produced under the pressure to meet quotas that help the foreman's future, not the customers. If sales are focused on selfish ambition, delivery dates will be promised that cannot possibly be kept, and this means that, when the protesting telephone calls come, assurance will be offered about finishing the task "next week," when everyone knows next month is the soonest it can happen. Perhaps one of the greatest evidences of selfish ambition in corporate America is the prevalent reality of what we might call "after flaws," problems left over and discovered after a manager has been promoted that he never dealt with and which he left behind for someone else to face. Often, these flaws don't show up until their perpetrator is two or three levels up the ladder, headed for bigger and better things. As a result, an innocent victim pays for the sins of the past while the perpetrator progresses on toward a fatter paycheck and greater power.

Sometimes company chaos costs more, even the very life of the one who brings it on. The tragic tale of Robert Edgell illustrates this.[9] Edgell, long successful in the publishing field, often worked out deals on the backs of cocktail napkins. He built up HBJ publications so it was making $12 million on revenues of $200 million a year. With such success, it was easy for him to lead a leveraged buyout of Harcourt Brace Jovanovich book publishers in a deal that *Fortune* calls "the definition of hubris." It is estimated that Edgell and partners paid $100 million too much and put HBJ in the helpless position of never being able to generate enough income to repay the debt. Once the major funder, Kidder Peabody, discovered this, they eased Edgell out as CEO and laid off dozens of employees, many of them Edgell's friends. After the company defaulted on a $7 million interest payment due on its bonds, Edgell began to behave in bizarre ways. Then, on New Year's Day 1991, he leaped off his Florida condo balcony seven stories to his death. He left behind five audio tapes for his family, and on one of them he said, "My way was wrong." Edgell has given us the ultimate summary of blind ambition.

SELF-MADE JUNK

But company chaos is only the first fruit of selfish ambition. As James continues, "every evil thing" is the second fruit and the more damaging. There is the evil of using people as pawns for the success of those moving up the ladder; the evil of taking advantage of trusting customers who may find out too late that they have been deceived and misled, sent shoddy products, and left in the lurch; the evil of destroying others by making them cheat and steal and lie. But there is another kind of evil in selfish ambition, the evil that turns its practitioners into junk, trash, garbage, hot dog wrappers.

James uses a unique word for evil in this passage, a word that has the root idea of something which is light and easily blown in the wind, something which is evil because it is useless, a piece of trash, of no value, a hunk of junk. People who are controlled by selfish ambition have as a lifetime product junk, garbage, trash, no matter how successful, famous, or rich they may be.

The word for evil reminds me of my boyhood days in Philadelphia, growing up as an ardent fan of the Phillies. Except for one burst of beauty in 1950 when we won the National League pennant, the Phillies were horrible, but they were my team. As I recall it, every time we played the then Brooklyn Dodgers we lost, and I hated the Dodgers because they were so good and we were so bad. When the Dodgers came to town I knew we were going to lose. In those days, the Phillies played at Scheib Park (later called Connie Mack Stadium), where there was a high, dark green fence in right field. Whenever Duke Snider, the Dodgers' all-star center fielder, came to bat, he seemed to take aim on that right field fence and delight in propelling the ball over it and onto the roofs of the houses across the street.

I remember being at Phillies-Dodgers games when, late in the game, about the seventh inning, with the Dodgers ahead 11–3, someone in the stands down by first base would decide to express his opinion of the Phillies by wadding up a hot dog wrapper and throwing it on the field. The piece of trash would land at the feet of the first baseman where the breeze would catch it and blow it across the infield to the dirt strip that used to run between the pitching mound and home plate. The scene would inevitably be set with the Duke up at bat in his characteristic left-handed stance. My hero was the catcher, number 21, Andy Seminick. Andy would be down in the crouch, the umpire bending down looking just over Andy's left shoulder, the pitcher about to start his motion—when the hot dog wrapper would make its appearance, catching Duke's attention.

Now Duke knew he could not focus on two white orbs at the same time, and he also knew that the hot dog wrapper was an imposter, a piece of garbage, and not the real thing. What Duke wanted to see was an official National League ball, not a piece of junk. So, as soon as he saw the hot dog wrapper, Duke straightened up, stepped out of his stance, turned and faced the umpire, and said, "Time out, Ump!" Immediately the umpire straightened up, stepped out of his stance, whipped off his mask, and yelled, "Time out!" Then he ran out from behind the plate up the dirt strip toward the pitcher's mound. Next he reached down, grabbed the hot dog wrapper, stuffed it in his pocket, and yelled, "Play ball!" Whereupon, the pitcher would pitch and Duke would hit his home run.

God treats selfishly ambitious people like umpires treat hot dog wrappers: He calls time out, removes them from the playing field, gets them out of the way of the game, and then gets life moving along. Selfishly ambitious people make themselves throw-away people in the game of life. Robert Young, for all he achieved, shows us this. So does Haman. And so, painfully, does Robert Edgell.

FROM A HOT DOG WRAPPER TO A STALLION

But what if we don't want to be a throw-away person in the game of life? What can we do about this? And what can we do with the feelings that ambition produces within, especially when we realize that these feelings are strongly self focused? How can we avoid becoming a hot dog wrapper in the game of life?

Thank God, He is in the business of transforming hot dog wrappers into stallions. Although ambition can be negative, it is not always so, as we discover when we realize there is positive ambition, an ambition that loves to honor God. The energy of ambition cannot be denied or willed away; it can, however, be transformed into a life-developing power rather than a life-destroying power. Ambition is like a river that rages in frightening annual floods which, when dammed, is transformed from a life-devastating flood to a life-supporting flow. When our ambition is transformed from selfish destruction to self-sacrificing dedication, we are transformed from hot dog wrappers to stallions, as we see from James.

When James asked who among us has the practical insight and essential knowledge to live life in a mature and fruitful way, he not only warns us about the twin killers of bitter jealousy and selfish ambition; he also exhorts us to meekness (James 3:12). Meekness is not a mark we aspire to, because we think of a meek person as a wallflower who has neither the commitment nor the courage to speak out or step forward. But this is not the meaning James had in mind when he exhorted us to such a response. Meekness, at one point in its history, had an honorable meaning which spoke of strength and valor, not of weakness and fear. This is how James uses this word.

Some years ago, my wife and I were in Salem, Oregon, and we were invited out for dinner on a farm, a gentleman kind of farm, with green grass and white picket fences and beautifully built barns. While we were waiting for dinner to be served, the owner's daughter Heather, a petite young woman in her early twenties, invited us to go with her to the barn to watch her train her show horse.

As we watched Heather lead her beautiful black stallion out of his stall, even in the dim light of the barn we could see the muscles rippling under his coat, and we knew he was strong. I almost wanted to say, "Sir!" in respect as soon as I saw him. Any creature this big and this strong had to be courageous. It wasn't long until we realized he was intelligent as well. After she brushed him down and put a blanket on him, the young trainer cinched up the saddle in preparation for a training session. However, before swinging into the saddle, Heather did a very strange thing. This young, gentle woman doubled up her fist, pulled back as hard as she could, and hit the stallion right in the belly. She was not being mean. You see, he had filled his stomach with extra air when she cinched the saddle, air which he planned to let out just as she mounted him, loosening the saddle, causing her to crash headlong onto the barn floor. That stallion was intelligent.

And it did not take any time at all to realize he also had conviction. As soon as Heather mounted him and led him out on to the training track, we could see this. The training track was dirt surrounded by a white picket fence with a grass infield. As she rode him, the stallion continuously veered to the left toward the fence, making a constant effort to brush her off. He had conviction that she was not going to teach him to be a show horse.

STRENGTH UNDER THE MASTER'S CONTROL

What will happen to that stallion once he learns to respond to his trainer? Will he lose any of his courage or his strength or his intelligence or his conviction? No! Rather, he will gain a new skill, a skill he has never had before, so he can achieve things he would never have done without becoming meek. He will learn to submit his strength to the hand of a master. This is what James means by meekness: strength under the Master's hand. It is this that transforms selfish ambition from a destructive raging river to a constructive flow of life. The Master's control is the dam that redirects our lives into maturity and fruitfulness. Just as the stallion loses none of his characteristics when he is domesticated, so we lose none of our drive once we are broken and controlled by the Lord. Ambition will continue to be within us, but it is redirected from a dominating appetite for self-advancement to a mature desire to please the Lord. In this, we are transformed from hot dog wrappers to stallions.

James helps us understand that there is nothing wrong with the energy of ambition; it is the motive that is the problem. If the aim of our ambition is inward and self-focused, it is a destructive force both in our lives and in the lives of others. But if our ambition is outward toward others on the Lord's behalf, it is a constructive force which brings honor to Christ.

This is exactly how another writer, Paul, describes positive ambition; he uses a word that means to love to honor, and the Lord is the object of that loving honor. Paul speaks of positive ambition this way: "Therefore also we have as our ambition . . . to be pleasing to Him. For we must all appear before the judgment seat of Christ . . . " (2 Corinthians 5:10–11). We have positive ambition when we direct our energy to excel toward the Lord and His honor, when we make His interests more important than our own, when we remember that He will evaluate all we do to determine whether it was for us or for Him. To have positive ambition, then, our goal must be to please the Lord.

GARBAGE CAN OR SHOW RING

But what can we do to avoid the garbage can and aim for the show ring? We understand that there's nothing wrong with the energy of ambition, but we can't always tell how we are aiming that energy. One of the earliest followers of Jesus was his cousin, John, known to us as the Baptist. John gives us one of the most important guidelines concerning ambition. One day a debate broke out between John's followers and one who was questioning them about their religious practices. They brought their debate to John and introduced the conversation with the following words: "Teacher, He who was with you beyond the Jordan, to whom you have borne witness, behold He is baptizing, and all are coming to Him" (John 3:26).

Nothing could be more challenging to an ambitious man than to learn his territory has been invaded by a competitor. Baptism belonged to John. He had pioneered the practice; no one had ever baptized in Israel before. Only proselytes to Judaism got baptized in those days, and they dipped themselves in the water. John was the first one to immerse others. Crowds came out from Jerusalem to the wilderness to see him, hear what he was saying, and be baptized by him. He was a folk hero, a national figure with an impressive following. Now along comes someone who is moving onto his turf. All used to come to him; now all are going to that upstart! How will he respond? Perhaps he will seek to get a corner on the baptism market. Maybe he will offer a better deal, perhaps require a lesser righteousness than his competitor.

He did none of these things. Instead, he responded with one of the greatest insights into ambition I have ever discovered when he says, "A man can receive nothing, unless it has been given him from heaven" (John 3:27). From this we realize two realities: (1) we can't get what God doesn't want to give us, and (2) we can't accomplish what God doesn't purpose for us. Interestingly, John added an important truth about ambition when he told his followers concerning Jesus, "He must increase, but I must decrease" (v. 30; NASB). At work, our goal cannot be primarily a promotion or pay increase, but that He increases in importance to us; Jesus must be the driving force behind what we do.

We cannot get a position God hasn't given us, no matter how hard we try. We can set our sights, push our way up the ladder, get within sight of our hope, maybe even get the title and the office, but it brings only hurt and grief. There will be pain in our souls, despair in our spirits, sorrow in our hearts. No one can have anything heaven has not already given him without losing more than he ever gained.

Likewise, we can't accomplish what God hasn't purposed for us. We can establish our aim, strive to succeed, lay our hands on it, but when we do, it turns to dust. It is vain, nothing more than a chasing after the wind, an emptiness that leaves us frustrated and filled with our own futility. None of us can accomplish anything heaven has not already given us, and if we try to force our way, we will only bring pain to our souls.

Because of this, we must choose to submit ourselves to the will and purpose of God for us. God's limit is a loving limit, the limit of Calvary, where God chose to hold nothing back. Can anyone who gave His most precious possession, His own Son, to die for those who hate Him plan anything but good for us? None of us would give ourselves, let alone our sons, for those who hate us, yet this is what God has done. And we must respond to His desire to love us by bringing our desires under the disciplined control of love and dedication to Him. This is how we turn from the garbage heap to aim for the show ring.

The question, however, is how do we do this? After all, John knew exactly what his role was; it had been revealed to his father by a direct word from heaven, outlining in great detail not only his role but his clothing style and diet. None of us has such clear direction from heaven. We have much less certain guidance which leaves a great deal more of the choice up to us. There are at least two principles to guide us: anything you must give up integrity to get cannot be from God, and anything you must destroy others to get cannot be from God. Integrity and love form the banks of the river of ambition with God's sovereignty forming the dam and controlling the flow. But are there any specifics which will help us in directing the aim of our ambition? And what about the damage we have already done through the pursuit of our own selfish ambition?

EXPANSIVE EXECUTIVES

When we pursue selfish ambition, we focus all our attention on ourselves and our driven needs for success. No matter how much we may say we're doing it for our mates, our families, the company, the good of our customers, or anyone else, when we are driven by selfish ambition, we are doing it for ourselves! We choose to live in a universe of one and only one. We make ourselves Number 1, god in our own little universe. When we are committed to expanding our power and our control over our environment, we cannot be committed to developing our relationships, no matter how precious we may protest they are to us. In business, leaders dedicated to expanding their own presence and impact, even though they mask it in terms of company goals and quarterly numbers, have been called expansive executives. When this is true of us, we don't seek to be connected with others; we don't want to be dependent upon others; we feel it is weakness to acknowledge our need for others.[10] This means we may play up to those over us, treat our peers as if they were of no value, and take advantage of those who report to us by failing to give them the credit they deserve or, even worse, by taking credit from them for ourselves. Clearly, these are unethical actions, which alienate others from us.

Perhaps the worse part about selfish ambition is how it blinds us. We are often unable to see what others see in us and choose to live in the self-imposed darkness of denial. Few people describe this reality more effectively than John Dean, author of *Blind Ambition*. Advisor to the president of the United States, he compromised truth in an attempt to aid President Nixon overcome the Watergate scandal and to advance his own star. When Dean thought he was reaching the top, he discovered he had sunk to the bottom. "Slowly, steadily, I would climb toward the moral abyss of the President's inner circle until I finally fell into it, thinking I had made it to the top just as I began to realize I had actually touched bottom."[11]

Often, this distortion impacts us most at home, where the same values and attitudes prevail, but where our mates may be equally blind and our children helpless victims of our myopic vision. Sometimes it is when our sons and daughters become immature mirrors of ourselves, mimicking our every value and bearing the undisguised fruit of our characters, that we find ourselves face-to-face with the undeniable product of a lifetime of self-centeredness. Only then do we realize the great pain our willful choices have brought to those whom we say we love the most.

As one wife of a driven ambitious man said, "In the office he was very much in control; he was removed from intimate relationships. It's the one area where he functions superbly. He doesn't have to worry about hurting anyone's feelings. He handles superficial working relationships really well, where they don't demand deep emotional give-and-take.... He thrived in the office; he wrapped his whole life there; it was a neat package. He didn't have to go beyond the office for anything."[12]

Listen to the pain in this woman's words. Imagine her feelings of not being needed, her fear of being overly sensitive, her frustration of having no intimacy with the man she married, whose children she bore. Think of what such a man has done to his wife. Does it surprise us that any who do this must grieve over the pain they have brought to those whom they vowed to love and cherish and whom they are responsible to nourish and guide to maturity?

Robert Kaplan, of the Center for Creative Leadership, America's premier leadership think tank, writing in *Beyond Ambition,* demonstrates this reality through a series of case studies designed to discover why promising young executives fail to fulfill their potential. All these studies come from the business world and are actual stories of living men and women who have fallen short of their promise in modern American corporations. These are not religious studies, and the impact of religion is either missing or totally incidental to the research Kaplan conducted. In Kaplan's studies the overwhelming testimony of men and women is that selfish ambition becomes a set of invisible shackles for them, blinding them to the impact of their self-centeredness, their most obvious flaw. It's as if they are enmeshed in a clinging Saran Wrap®. Those looking at them from the outside can see their potential if only they were free to be themselves, but their own dark drive holds them, limiting their reach, so they cannot grasp all that could be theirs if they were free. Responses made by peers, subordinates, mates, and children cannot penetrate their self-imposed deafness, so they neither see nor hear until it's too late. What could have been never will be because of this blinding and deafening hardness of heart.

Kaplan gives a devastating list of selfish ambition's marks.[13] We will do well to study it carefully and ask others to critique us ruthlessly concerning these destructive characteristics.

Overreaching strategically
Being risk-averse
Running roughshod over subordinates
Being cold and aloof
Focusing on empire building and other kinds of self-aggrandizement
Being inordinately concerned with getting ahead
Not distinguishing clearly enough between high- and low-priority items
Pushing themselves too hard and burning out
Pushing people too hard and burning them out
Being rigid or difficult to influence
Being too concerned with status symbols, trappings of power, and the like
Not delegating enough
Having an inflated sense of their own importance
Distorting reality to create a favorable impression
Generally lacking integrity

FORWARD TOWARD FREEDOM

How do we respond if we realize our selfish ambition not only is keeping us from becoming all God created us to be, but also hurting those around us? I suggest five responses which will help us move forward in our freedom to serve others and not ourselves.

1. Grieve over any pain your selfish ambition has caused.

We must grieve for the pain we have caused those whom we vowed to love and cherish and whom we are responsible to nourish and guide to maturity. And then we must act to change at the core of our beings. Such change is not possible without grace from God and accountability from His people, because we cannot change in ourselves without both inner and outer help. In fact, Kaplan saw very little success in those who finally saw this fatal flaw and attempted to change.[14] Selfish ambition appears to be the Mount Everest of character change. Seemingly monumental, the peak called ambition can be overcome by recognizing it is there and asking God's help to conquer it.

If you have a family, grieve at the rejection you have expressed to your children because you have made your career, i.e., your security, more important than their security and, by so doing, you have passed your insecurity on to them in what may turn out to be a more heightened form. Grieve over the pain you have brought your mate because you have given so little of yourself and your time to your marriage and kept so much of yourself for yourself. Grieve for the lost hours of joy and delight and discovery you will never know with your mate. Grieve because of the frustration and confusion that is the legacy you have given to your marriage.

Whether married or single, grieve over the way you have deceived your superiors by making them think you are a loyal employee when, in fact, you are only loyal to yourself. You are not serving them but using them in an effort to get ahead.

Grieve over the way you have disregarded your peers and inwardly thought yourself superior to them, better executive/leadership material, more inherently deserving of advancement than they. You may have been driven to compete with them, to defeat them, to disregard them, to care about them only when it is useful to you. Your attitudes and actions may have generated feelings of anger and resentment in them.

Grieving involves repentance. Recognize the hurt you may have caused family and coworkers with your disregard. If you are a manager, you may need to grieve over the way you have taken advantage of those who report to you, using them for your interests without caring very much about theirs. They may well have come to recognize as false and misleading your insincere expressions of concern and compassion. For that you must grieve and repent of such attitudes.

Most of all, grieve over your refusal to trust God for your career path, for your independent self-reliance which reflects your fear that God doesn't know what you need. Deep down inside you may feel that God's will is not good enough for you because God may not want you to be as successful as you are driven to be. Humble yourself before God and acknowledge the pride which has caused you to be your own god. Selfish ambition reduces us to the least we can be, our own gods, victims of a self-deluding idolatry.

When we are so driven by the fear that God will not give us what we feel we so desperately need, we miss the greatness of what God intends for us: a joyous marriage, friendships, and the satisfaction of achievements that glorify Him, whether that means a place at the top and a lucrative income or service at a lower level. Grieve because you have distrusted God, the one who gave His most precious possession, His Son, to die for you and live in you. Grieve over years wasted worshiping at the empty shrine of self.

2. Entrust your life-dream to God.

Make the choice to trust God for all you dream of accomplishing. Believe that God wants good for you; in fact, He wants the best for you. Trust God's loving intentions for you enough to let Him determine what your success should be. Act to obey Him, no matter what.

Take those driven feelings, those demanding desires for power, recognition, and honor, and bring them to Him so He can transform them into desires to serve others. Learn to recognize any signs of self-centered control marking you: the constant focus on how good you are, the anger at being slighted, the competitive feelings toward others who have the same dreams you have or to whom you credit the same dreams. Learn to listen to those who are close to you. Hear their pleas for time from you, for encouragement from you, for attention when they talk to you, for you to listen and take an interest in their concerns. Give them the recognition they deserve. Pay attention to your critics; take them seriously and seek to bring about the changes they call for in you by God's power. Determine that your life's dream will be obeying God no matter what He wants.

Then sit down and develop a life dream for yourself. It may well be that God has implanted a dream in your heart which He will give you if you will give it to Him. If you could chart your own course, what would it look like? CEO of a corporation? Owner of your own company? Researcher in a lab? National sales manager? Service on a design engineering team? For some, success means the top position, the challenge and delight of steering the ship through difficult economic storms. Others, though, don't want anything to do with the management chain. For them, that's exactly what management is, a chain, in fact, a ball-and-chain which keeps them from their dreams of making a contribution through planning or product development or sales.

What is your dream? Think through what has brought you challenge and pleasure in the past. Go all the way back to your childhood, because it is here that we first begin to express our giftedness. How has God made you? What did He make you to achieve and enjoy? What have you done already in life that confirms this? What are your greatest areas of strength? What will you never be good at doing? Put all of this thinking about yourself together and design a position in which your capacities could be used to the maximum. Remember that the younger you are, the less likely you are to have an accurate view of yourself. No matter how old you are, also remember that God may have exciting and unexpected surprises in store for you. Once you have come up with your dream position, pray about it and take the steps you can by serving others rather than seeking for yourself. It just may be what God Himself has designed for you. Trust Him and see what He does. But be certain you *entrust your life-dream to God.*

3. Give God your time.

Make the conscious choice to give God your time to do with as He pleases. Throughout most of our lives, God leaves the choice of what we do with our time to us. Thus we are responsible to determine whether we will use it to obey Him or serve ourselves. The call I issue here is to a total releasing of our time to God's purposes, so our life-dream becomes obeying Him as consistently as possible. Although perfection is not achievable, dedicated effort toward God's perfect standard through dependence on His Holy Spirit must be our daily pursuit.

So now when we plan to achieve our life dream, our question is not what we want to do with our time but how do we organize our schedule so we move toward growing obedience? This will lead to at least some of the following questions:

How can I plan my schedule so a regular slice of my time is dedicated exclusively to Him?

How can I plan my schedule so I am loving and responding to my mate in the way God intends?

How can I plan my schedule so I am nurturing my children in Christ and passing on to them both the faith to which I am committed and the emotional support and encouragement they need from me as their parent?

How can I plan my schedule so I make the income my family needs without making wealth my true god?

How can I plan my schedule so I serve others rather than using them? How can I plan my schedule so I help my superiors become more effective? How can I plan time into my schedule for my peers so I serve them and help them achieve their goals? How can I plan time in my schedule for my subordinates so I serve them by expressing interest and concern for their needs and interests?

Perhaps you have noticed that the approach to time I am taking at this point is not oriented so much to activities as it is to values. If we want our ambition to turn us into stallions, we must focus our time on values rather than functions. If we value God, we will focus our time on Him; if we value marriage, we will focus our time on our mates; if we value family, we will focus our time on our children; if we value our fellow employees, we will focus our time on them in accordance with both their functional and personal needs. One of the greatest measures of our true values is found in our daily calendars. As you finish reading this chapter, write down your values. Next, reschedule your time so your calendar becomes a record of the achievement of your values. Then commit to entrust your time to God to invest it in accomplishing what He values, not what you have valued up until now.

4. Find significance through relationships, not just achievements.

We are born to relate first and achieve second; God created us to relate in a family first and then to work in His world. Without relationships, achievements leave us empty and unfulfilled, yet, in our desire to relate, we cannot overlook our built-in need for achievement. God made us to work, to express His image and likeness in service to Him and others. However, because we have lost our original sense of purpose as well as our ability to love freely as God intended, we tend to substitute achievements for relationships, i.e., we try to draw from our achievements what only healthy relationships can give us. This is why we focus on achieving our selfish dreams rather than sacrificing ourselves in loving and serving others. We think that achievements can give us the feelings of security and value which we so desperately crave, but only healthy relationships can fulfill these longings.

The problem is that relationships threaten us, make us feel uncomfortable, and bring fear into our lives. We can't control relationships, and we can't hide in relationships. Friends talk back to us, hold us accountable, reflect ourselves back to us, tear down our walls, and force us to face our flaws. This is the problem with mates and children. They won't allow us to hide our fears or deny our flaws or avoid vulnerability. They make us look at ourselves whether we like it or not. But we can't face being so totally revealed, so we react to protect ourselves by avoiding relationships and focusing on achievements.

Men and women buried in achievements may find temporary success but neither lasting satisfaction or true identity. Achievements give us a false sense of identity, the feeling that we are somebody when we may well be denying all aspects of our personhood. If we are using the people at work, taking advantage of our mates, and ignoring our children, we are failures as human beings, no matter what we achieve on the job. Healthy human beings have healthy human relationships! Healthy human relationships are not perfect human relationships; there will be confusion, tension, and disappointment in the very best relationships because we are human and scarred by sin. But there are healthy ways to deal with these struggles, ways that produce healing and harmony. And even where healing and harmony do not come, we can fulfill our responsibility before God by doing our best to bring this about in obedience to His truth.

Thus, the measure of human health is in our relationships, not in our achievements. Relationships form the context in which achievements take on their greatest meaning and contribution; relationships energize true achievement, because they give us healthy feelings of confidence and value as well as the sensitivity necessary to see what we need to achieve to meet the needs of others.

To commit ourselves to find significance from relationships, not just achievements, we must commit ourselves to face our greatest fears, our deepest insecurities, and our highest walls, for we can never relate until we do this. This will mean learning to listen, to hear what those around us say to us about the barriers we raise to block them out and keep ourselves within our protective barricades. Until we initiate an open door policy concerning our inner beings toward those who live and work with us and have a need to relate to us, we shall always be looking for significance from achievements; once we allow others to touch us and tell us what they feel inside of us, we can begin to know the wonder of the way God created us.

5. Walk by the Spirit.

There is no way apart from God's enabling power that we can take any of the steps needed to release ourselves from the bondage of selfish ambition to the beauty of serving ambition. If we will (1) grieve for our failures, (2) entrust our life-dream to God, (3) evaluate our time according to our values, (4) and seek significance through achievements in the context of healthy relationships, we will see the greatest release from the bondage of pride we have ever seen in our lives. We will cease being hot dog wrappers. But the transformation into strong, healthy stallions happens only with God's help. The inner forces of resistance which grip us are too great for us to break in our own resources. This is why we need to depend on the Holy Spirit and His enablement for our freedom.

To walk by the Spirit is to rely on the Spirit for each step of life: for each moral decision, each ethical decision, each relational decision, each personal decision, each vocational decision. To walk by the Spirit demands, first, that we know what God wants us to do in each of these decision clusters, which means we must know God's Word in such a way that we understand what we must do to obey Him. At times, this will be difficult to discern because the issues are not always as sharp and clear as we would like them to be. There will be many occasions when we must turn for help to like-minded friends and counselors and, even then, we may have to take some uncertain steps because the way is not clear to us. But even in the clearest of situations we are not able to obey God on our own.

It takes the Holy Spirit's enablement to be obedient to God and His Word. This is why we must walk by the Spirit.

Reliance on the Holy Spirit is a mental attitude of trust in which I consciously count on Him and His indwelling presence to enable me to do what God wants me to do. He indwells all believers and makes His enabling power available to all who trust Him. Thus, when I fear a relationship, but I know He wants me to love those involved, I trust Him for the capacity to love; when I fear an assignment, but I know He wants me to accomplish it, I trust Him for the capacity to achieve the task. I consciously rely upon Him to do what only His supernatural power can achieve.

My wife's grandmother, Grandma Little, lived to be ninety-six years old, and, late in her life, we could see her physical strength literally draining away. For the last several years of her life, she lived at a nursing home called Pilgrim Haven, five minutes from my in-laws' home. Whenever we had a family event, it was our responsibility to bring Grandma Little to my in-laws' house. Every time we did that, the same chain of events occurred. My wife and I would pull up in front of Pilgrim Haven and go in for Grandma Little. She would be ready for us, sitting in her favorite chair, her shawl wrapped around her, a smile on her face. I would ask, "How are you, Grandma?" And she would always reply, "Pretty good, Bill." Then I would offer her my arm, assist her out of her chair, and we'd walk down the long hallway, out the front door, down the steps, out the gate, and into our car. Grandma Little, who was incapable of walking on her own, walked by the power of Bill Lawrence by relying on my enabling energy. And always she would say the same thing: "Now don't go too fast, Bill!"

That's the way walking by the Holy Spirit works. We have no power in ourselves to perceive the pain we cause others, let alone grieve for it; on our own we do not have enough confidence in God to entrust our life-dreams to Him; we are unable to control our time according to our values; we do not have enough security to enter into in-depth relationships. We must walk by the Spirit if we are to become stallions and escape being hot dog wrappers. The physical picture of Grandma Little walking through my energy helps me understand the spiritual reality of my walking by the Spirit's energy.

BEYOND THE BOTTOM LINE

*I*t is only the Holy Spirit who can take you beyond the bottom line to the foundation of your life. He knows the way to the hidden secrets of your being, to the locked closet where only God can carry you. He will help you evaluate the motives of your ambition. He will help you recognize selfish ambition and jealousy. He will guide you in establishing new values through God's Word. Here, the Spirit will enable you to make new commitments, commitments that will deliver you from an insensitive self-focus to a care for others you have never known. The Spirit will teach you to rebuild your beliefs in the light of the Bible so you see yourself as God sees you, and so you can see others with His eyes.

This takes time, a lifetime, in fact, of growing and learning to think clearly and to live with others, not self. But remember, stallions grow strong over time, with exercise, occasional missteps, and close listening to the master's words, as the stallion on that Oregon farm listened to Heather.

And this is my hope for you. If you will walk by the Spirit, you will be released from the invisible shackles of selfish ambition to become one whose ambition is to serve others, the very thing that turns us all from hot dog wrappers into stallions. What could be greater?

CHAPTER NINE

IF YOU'RE LEGAL, YOU'RE RIGHT

Can you swim with the sharks and still be ethical? Or do you need to be two different people to succeed in business: Mr. Nice Guy at home and Mr. Mean Guy at the office? Do the rules of the road change when you get into the fast lane or is the speed limit the same for all?

Some believe that business people need two sets of ethics just as most of us have two kinds of cars, a family car for outings with our mates and children and a work car that we drive to and from the office each day. For some, ethics are like having two cars, one set for the family and one set for the job.

Whether you agree with that perspective or not, you certainly model it if you teach your children to tell the truth at home while you bend the truth in negotiations. Indeed, some teach their children to love each other at home while they seek to destroy others in the business world. They tell their wives to be forthright with friends while they practice deception in their businesses.

Thus we must ask ourselves one very practical question: Should business ethics and personal ethics be consistent, or are there two different standards, one for personal relationships and one for business success? Consider, for example, the business practice of bluffing. Is bluffing ethical? Can you bluff about your bottom price during sales negotiations and obey God? Must you deceive when you bluff? What role does threat have in bluffing?

ETHICAL BLUFFING

In an article in the *Harvard Business Review* entitled "Is Business Bluffing Ethical?" business consultant Albert Z. Carr answered the question by arguing that business and personal ethics are different. According to the article, personal ethics do not apply to business so that business people must leave their personal ethics at home when they come to the office.

> The basis of private morality is a respect for truth and . . . the closer a businessman comes to the truth, the more he deserves respect. At the same time, . . . most bluffing in business might be regarded simply as game strategy—much like bluffing in poker, which does not reflect on the morality of the bluffer.[1]

Carr quotes Henry Taylor, a British statesman, who asserted that "falsehood ceases to be falsehood when it is understood on all sides that the truth is not expected to be spoken—an exact description of bluffing in poker, diplomacy, and business."[2] In other words, if everyone knows everyone else is lying, then nobody is lying, and this is exactly what it means to bluff. Concerning the use of the bluff, Carr says, "Whatever the form of the bluff, it is an integral part of the game, and the executive who does not master its techniques is not likely to accumulate much money or power."[3] According to this argument, business is a game, and it should be understood this way. It is for this reason that business ethics are different from personal ethics.

> The justification [that business ethics must be different from personal ethics] rests on the fact that business, as practiced by individuals as well as by corporations, has the impersonal character of a game—a game that demands both special strategy and an understanding of its special ethics.[4]

PLAYING BY THE RULES

According to Carr, business is a game with its own set of rules and ethics. Therefore, business requires a special ethic based on strategy of what is good for the bottom line, not what is right or wrong.

Business is our main area of competition, and it has been ritualized into a game of strategy. The basic rules of the game have been set up by the government, which attempts to detect and punish business frauds. But as long as a company does not transgress the rules of the game set by law, it has the legal right to shape its strategy without reference to anything but its profits. If it takes a long-term view of its profits, it will preserve amicable relations, so far as possible, with those with whom it deals. A wise businessman will not seek advantage to the point where he generates dangerous hostility among employees, competitors, government, or the public at large. But decisions in this area are, in the final test, *decisions of strategy, not of ethics.*[5]

Based on this, Carr states that ethics are valuable as long as they are profitable. But if ethics get in the way of profit, they must go.

THE ISSUE: PRIVATE ETHICS VS. POKER ETHICS

Think a moment about Carr's argument and his ominous conclusion. Profits supersede ethics. Carr argues that business is different from other elements of life because business is a game like poker, with which it has much in common.

He acknowledges that rules exist in poker—there are poker ethics. You can't play with a marked deck, or deal from the bottom of the deck, or plant someone to look over your opponent's shoulder and send you signals about his hand. These actions will get you thrown out of the game—or even shot.

Just as there are laws in poker, so there are laws for business, laws that must be observed, and, according to Carr, as long as you are legal you are right! All you're responsible to do is to keep the law and make a profit. A business is an entity that exists to make a profit within the law, concurs the eminent economist Milton Friedman of the University of Chicago. Therefore, if you're legal and profitable you're ethical, no matter what happens to your employees, your customers, or your neighbors because of your actions.

Unless you see reality this way you will not succeed either in poker or business. "Violations of the ethical ideals of society are common in business, but they are not necessarily violations of business principles,"[6] Carr writes. One executive, accused of using a harmful substance in a mouthwash his company produced, declared to a congressional investigative panel,

We don't make the laws. We obey them. Then why do we have to put up with this "holier than thou" talk about ethics? It's sheer hypocrisy. We're not in business to promote ethics. . . . If the ethics aren't embodied in the laws by the men who made them, you can't expect businessmen to fill the lack. Why, a sudden submission to Christian ethics by businessmen would bring about the greatest economic upheaval in history![7]

Obviously, according to this assertion, integrity has no voice in business beyond the law; further, there is no guarantee that the law will always be just. All too often, the law is subject to political influence, and that hardly guarantees justice for all. Granted, a person may be torn by the tension between personal and business ethics, but those who advocate a pragmatic ethic of profits above all else argue "the sooner we make peace with reality the healthier we'll be when it comes to business."

Carr's own words summarize the argument effectively. "If a man plans to take a seat in the business game, he owes it to himself to master the principles by which the game is played, including its special ethical outlook."[8] When it comes to business, the bottom line reigns supreme, and there is just one rule: do whatever you can, however you can, as long as it's legal to get as much as you can. If you don't understand this rule or can't play for its stakes, don't get into the game because you can't afford to lose.

I wonder, though, how those who agree with Carr would like it if a vendor took a "poker" approach to negotiations over a shortage of critical materials. Or what happens when a customer tries to bluff or play by his own set of rules when it comes to wording a critical long-term contract? Eventually the vendor's hand would be called, he has to show his cards. When his cards are less than implied, there's a sudden cry for consistency, for the same kind of ethics on the job as at home. When it comes to a customer, though, even if the company knows it's being bluffed, they may not do much about it, because the customer has so much economic leverage. Just because the customer wins, however, doesn't make his ethical approach right.

ROGUE RULES

What, then, does this mean to us as Christians? Is business really a game with its own set of rogue rules, a unique kind of ethics that includes deception and bluffing and excludes personal standards of conscience? When we view business as a game in which the players play by a unique set of rules different from those by which everyone else lives, we take a narrow and short-sighted view, certainly not the view God takes—the view that people matter and long-term consequences count. This latter view is a healthy one, so we must play the game of business according to God's rules, not "poker" rules. Business and morality *cannot* be separated;

they're directly linked. Both the ancient teachings of God and the modern realities of Western morality show this to be true.

TOTAL ETHICS

From God's ancient teachings we learn that He is consistent in what He says, not only about business but about every area of life. God does not have one set of ethics for the home and another for the office; He calls for total righteousness in all relationships and activities of life wherever these occur. God commands us to tell the truth without exception[9], while He describes those who tell lies as treacherous and warns that they will not escape punishment (Proverbs 14:25; 19:5). He owns the just scale and declares that "all the weights of the bag are his concern" (Proverbs 16:11). He tells us that when we pursue treasures with a lying tongue we actually pursue a fleeting vapor, death itself (Proverbs 21:6). Instead, we are to work obediently and enthusiastically because the Lord is our boss; God commands us to work heartily for the Lord's reward, not just for human reward (Colossians 3:22–23, 25). The temptation to lie and deceive over money is so great that the writer of Proverbs prays that God will protect the truth teller by keeping lies and deception far from him (30:8). The power of wealth is far greater than the power of our wills, and we will fall prey to its attraction without God's enablement. A number of additional passages found in Proverbs show how strongly God feels about issues of ethics and integrity in business.[10] Once you look at these passages, you will know God does not have two different sets of ethics.

This means that the only way we can do business is by faith, by trusting God for His power and wisdom. We please Him because we value His will more than we do our wealth. At times, perhaps much of the time, good ethics will translate into good business, but more than one person who has put God's will ahead of personal wealth found himself out of work, without income, black-balled by those with lesser ethics who think him a fool for letting the truth stand in the way of a profit. Those who dismiss the ethical worker may chide him for his virtue: "Oh, come on, everyone knew what was being said in the negotiations wasn't actually true anyway."

TO TELL THE TRUTH

What do God's rules for business require? What is the righteous thing to do when it comes to telling the truth, for example? Does it mean we must tell all the truth all the time, or is there a need-to-know wisdom guideline that helps us determine what and how much of the truth to tell? Aren't there valid reasons why we don't tell all of the truth all of the time?

At times withholding all information about a product or procedure is acceptable. A legitimate need does exist to protect against industrial espionage or to defend against patent infringement, for instance, or to withhold information that would hurt one's business from others, or to hold back knowledge that others do not have a right to know. Everyone may not agree with your decision, of course, and some may accuse you of lying or deceiving, but if you are convinced they have either no right or no need to know, you are morally obligated to withhold information, no matter how much they may want to know it or how angry they become if they discover it.

But this is not playing the game according to some sort of special "poker" rules. This is playing the game exactly as Jesus played it when He told His disciples, "I have many more things to say to you, but you cannot bear them now" (John 16:12 NASB). His disciples had neither a right nor a need to know the things Jesus had not yet told them because they were not prepared for such knowledge. Some day they will know these things, but not at that time. But to maintain their trust and prepare them adequately for the future, Jesus told them the truth: "I've told you all I can, but there is still more coming." His action is loving, righteous, and ethical. This is the way we need to respond if we are to earn and maintain the trust of others.

Certainly we must respond to direct questions with direct answers, as Alan B. Potter, vice president of the Ciba Company Limited, comments:

> ... it is not at all the case that businessmen do not expect the truth to be spoken. On the contrary, almost all day-to-day business is conducted verbally on the basis of nonlegal documents. The economic system would collapse without mutual trust on a practically universal scale among business executives. ... Businessmen know that it would be ridiculous to expect anything more than a straight answer to a straight question. Moreover, it is perfectly acceptable to withhold the truth by saying , "I am sorry, I am not willing to discuss that subject." There are many reasons of self-interest or discretion which would justify a refusal to answer any question, and businessmen do not expect that those reasons need to be given.[11]

The best business relationships exist where ethical negotiations occur in an atmosphere of straight forward bargaining, in which all involved understand that each is looking for the best deal. Of course, the best deal is a deal in which everyone is satisfied to the degree this is possible and no one feels fleeced. Businessmen and women who want to stay in business know this and act accordingly. And they know this because they understand business and morality cannot be separated. No one will last long in business with two sets of ethics, one for home and one for work. Sooner or later the innate hypocrisy of this ethical version of riding the Roman horse will throw us and reduce our society, business and all, to its lowest common denominator. Indeed, looking at American morality today we can see that this is exactly what is happening in the marketplace and elsewhere.

NO POKER ETHIC

Clearly, we must not allow a conflict between private and public morality. We cannot have a personal ethic at home and a poker ethic in the office. When we separate business and personal ethics we begin to shatter the essence of our society. In fact, what has happened in business ethics is determining what is happening in personal ethics; and this, in turn, is having a further effect on business. Where a wild card ethic rules in business, it also takes over our private lives, and returns again to impact our business lives in an even more powerful way. What we are facing in these days is a circle, a rapidly closing, downward spiraling circle, in which the deterioration of ethics in the public sector, including politics, religion, entertainment, and business, brings an even more precipitous decline of ethics in our private lives, which will reach out to haunt our manufacturing sites and office suites. Let me show you what I mean.

LIFE: A MUST WIN GAME

In recent years, we have seen the result of a growing "poker" ethic in our society, as more and more of us approach life as a game that we must win. Life has become a wild pursuit in which men and women play for higher and higher stakes as they gamble away every form of ethical idealism in order to triumph at any price. To use our gambling analogy further, such attitudes have resulted in executives who are using marked cards, hiding cards up the sleeves, or making even more blatant moves. Men and women in every area of life will pay any price they must to get all the chips they think they need.

Look at this list of well-known and well-respected names in our society and think of what they have in common.

Business: Salomon Brothers, BCCI, Lincoln Savings, Drexel Burnham Lambert, Nichael Milken, Dennis Levine, Leona Helmsley, and Charles Keating.

Nonprofit and academic: United Way of America and Stanford University.

Religion: Jimmy Swaggart, Jim Bakker, Robert Tilton, other influential national and local spiritual leaders, and accusations of child molesting by priests.

Government: Joseph Biden, Gary Hart, the House of Representatives Bank Post Office scandal, Speaker of the House Jim Wright, presidential aide John Sununu, Mayor Marion Barry of Washington, D.C., and FBI director William Sessions.

Entertainment and sports: rock stars Milli Vanilli, James Brown, Mike Tyson, Pete Rose, Ben Johnson, and football stars Lawrence Taylor and Dexter Manley. [12]

The one thing that all of the names on this list have in common is that each has been at least sullied by some substantial charge of ethical breakdown. Many have been forced to confess their shame publicly, still others have been held accountable for their unethical activities, with their punishment ranging from suspension (e.g., SMU football, football star Dexter Manley) and banishment (sprinter Ben Johnson) to loss of recognition (rock group Milli Vanilli, whose stars didn't actually sing their music), denial of potential high office (Joseph Biden, Gary Hart), bankruptcy and cessation of business (Drexel Burnham Lambert), the shaking of public confidence (the United Way of America, whose president misspent funds) and to the conviction and imprisonment (Charles Keating, Michael Milken, Dennis Levine, Leona Helmsley, James Brown, Jim Bakker). Some may have been accused and shamed falsely as part of a political or personal vendetta as several claimed (the Keating Five, William Sessions). Others, spiritual leaders in particular, have been proven to be hypocrites of the highest order, often preaching or even writing about marriage and morality while engaging in ongoing immorality.

UNPARALLELED ETHICAL FAILURE

An unparalleled outburst of ethical failure has fallen upon us with an intensity and impact never equaled in the history of our nation. So many have played the game of life the poker way—bid, bluff, deceive, hide, call, cover, feign friendliness in order to mislead—that lying has become almost a way of life in our society. *Time* put it best in a cover story on lying when it declared, "Everyone's doin' it. (Honest)." The article describes the current political atmosphere of distrust as "a pervasive sense of moral moonscape where authority ought to reign. Everyone in power lies, the current wisdom runs, and those who are caught lying either don't care or tell more lies in order to clear themselves.[13]

An unprecedented stain of shameful scandal has struck in our day, a veritable tidal wave of dishonesty sweeping across our land. In 1991, the

Department of Justice boasted that they prosecuted and convicted 1,150 public officials, the highest number in any one year of American history.[14] These were not accusations; these were convictions. In the late 1980s there were more spy scandals than in all of American history combined.[15] And this doesn't take into account the often mentioned S&L scandals and the record billions of dollars they have cost the country. Michael Josephson, who has researched the ethical attitudes of those who are currently eighteen to thirty years old, declares that more scandals occurred among major political, business, sports, and religious leaders in the 1980s than in the prior five decades combined.[16] "In the trenches of politics, business, sports and journalism, simple notions of honesty and fair play were distorted or abandoned. Individual moral responsibility was often replaced by the idea that, if it's legal it's ethical."[17] Colson declares that there "is a crisis of character: a loss of those inner restraints and virtues that prevent Western civilization from pandering to its own darkest instincts."[18] Because we have turned from our Judeo-Christian moorings, we have lost our national heart and soul, and "no society can survive without a moral consensus."[19] Today, the United States leads the world in the rate of incarceration per capita for one reason: "We've lost our moral consensus. We're a people living for ourselves."[20]

Some may feel that this assessment is too dark, that the sky is cloudy but not midnight black. Certainly not everyone has fallen from grace, not all are unethical. Floyd Wilkerson, retired administrative vice president of Eaton Corporation, who also spent several years in key positions with TWA, including ten years as a vice president, told me that never once was he asked to lie by either company. A man of impeccable ethical standards, Wilkerson never had pressure put on him to compromise or dilute his convictions in any area of morality. Undoubtedly, there are many other corporations in the United States and around the world with the same unshakable standards. No, not everyone is unethical, but more are now than in the past, and their transgressions are greater than in previous periods. Something has happened at the ethical foundation of our land, and Colson's analysis is accurate: there is a crisis of character; we have lost our heart and soul; we cannot survive without a moral consensus. The whole body does not have to be sick for death to occur; cancer patients die despite a perfectly healthy heart and brain because the liver or the lung or something else is attacked and destroyed.

There is an ethical cancer loose in our land, and even though many, if not most in business are ethically healthy, we can still die if we do not choose to face and fight this malignant disease.

HANG ON TO YOUR LIFE JACKETS

So I hold to my assertion that there is a tidal wave of dishonesty sweeping our land. And what happens when we look past this surge to see what's coming next? Well, hang onto your life jackets because there's an even bigger wave coming. During the past three decades the family has undergone a steady deterioration; meanwhile, violent rejection of authority (the 1960s), hypocrisy (the 1970s), and gross greed (the 1980s) have chipped away at America's standards, even as television, with its twin lies of sitcom solutions and instant gratification, has expanded its influence. As a result, a significant number of those coming of age in the 1990s plan to play according to poker ethics. Their aim is clear: they will raise the ante until they've run the bid up higher than ever. Josephson declares that an analysis of values, beliefs, goals, and behavior of American youth from ages eighteen to thirty shows undeniable signs that our nation's moral fiber is weakening. Once this generation takes its place as decision makers in our society, the situation is likely to get worse.[21] Here are some specifics to back up his point, disturbing findings from recent studies and surveys.

Cheating. Almost three of every four high school students and one of every two college students admit to cheating, and the amount of cheating has been increasing in recent years. Other researchers suggest cheating rates may be as high as 87 percent, and with detection rates as low as 1.3%, cheaters win.[22]

Résumé fraud. As much as 24 percent of résumés present materially false information.[23] During an investigation on lying in America, the CBS television program interviewed Karen, a one-time disc jockey in Philadelphia who lied on her résumé to get her job. She defended her action, saying, "I lied on my résumé. Show me an actress who hasn't lied on her résumé, and I'll show you a waitress." The president of Fidelafacts, a firm that searches résumés for fraud, told a *48 Hours* reporter, "If people didn't lie, we would be out of business." In their résumé searches, Fidelafacts investigators find that about one-third of people lie in an effort to get a job. Perhaps they have Karen's attitude: it's OK to lie as long as no one gets hurt. However, since Karen was on radio and received newspaper publicity as a result, both her station and the *Philadelphia Inquirer*, her current employer, were hurt by her action because their credibility was on the line.[24]

Teenage pregnancies and sexual assaults. There are about one million teenage pregnancies annually and nearly 400,000 end in abortions, which means that 600,000 teenagers become mothers each year. Further, more than one college woman in four has been the victim of attempted or accomplished date rape and one survey of college men revealed that 50 percent said they would force a woman to have sex if they could get away with it.[25]

Crime. No other group in history has committed as many crimes against each other and their teachers as the current generation of eighteen- to thirty-year-olds.[26] There were almost three million incidents of attempted or completed assault, rape, robbery, or theft inside schools or on school property during the 1986–1987 school year. Many muggings and murders occur in an effort to get some piece of coveted sportswear.[27]

Josephson concludes "A very substantial number of young adults are entering or advancing in the work force with a disposition toward behaviors that are bound to endanger business and society."[28] But what else can we expect in light of the models which they have seen during their formative years? It's little wonder that they are committed to expediency; as one college junior said,

> Cheating is such an easy thing to do because everyone wants to be good and best and the only thing that measures that, in school at least, are grades. [When] you look at everything that is going on in the corporate world . . . it seems to be that the person that gets done first is the best. I think that it is hard to think of having morals when you hear all these stories about these people that don't have morals and are making big money.[29]

The under-thirty generation simply mirrors a massive shift in American values, although they accept these new values in higher proportions and perhaps greater intensity. Consider the following changes in values from the 1950s to 1980s[30]

1950s	1980s
Production	Consumption
Future gratification	Immediate gratification
Sacrifice	Greed
Public interest	Self-interest
Quality	Quantity
Long-term focus	Short-term focus

As we move toward the beginning of the twenty-first century we see that Western morality has a floating decimal point. Nothing is fixed in Western moral thought; whatever feels good is good. This has led to an ethical breakdown filtering from generation to generation until we have reached a point in which the current college and high school population stand at one of the lowest ethical ebbs in our history. Influenced by the negative models that lie before them, young adults are learning well from their elders as they advance toward positions of influence and power. The question we must now face is: what do we do about this? What *can* we do about this? We must respond by going beyond the bottom line.

— BEYOND THE BOTTOM LINE —

*W*e go beyond the bottom line by taking a stance against this encroaching army of me-first, satisfaction-at-any-cost young men and women. In doing so, we should not act out of anger toward the ones who might take us to a new ethical low, but out of concern—concern for the well-being of our nation and concern for the well-being of this new generation. These men and women need compassion, patience, accountability, and a taste of the spiritual reality they so obviously crave.

The answer is to become models, quiet heroes who bring with them a new morality and a new ethic. Such an ethic actually is a return to the ancient unchanging absolutes of the ages. Such men and women become models for the young who have rarely, if ever, seen anyone take a sacrificial stance for the right and the good.

Like Jack Turpin, Doug Rice, Norm Miller, and Floyd Wilkerson, these men and women for all seasons stand committed to the call of ethical excellence no matter what the price. Because of this, they become moral models, not only for younger generations, but for their peers as well. This is the decision you must make during your time. What those men have meant in their sphere of influence, you can mean in yours. No matter where you are in your corporation, from the highest rung of responsibility to the lowest level of influence, you can call others to commitment by standing committed yourself.

What does such a commitment look like? In the next chapter, we will consider three practical guidelines for an ethical lifestyle that models a full commitment to moral integrity.

CHAPTER TEN

GUIDELINES FOR ETHICS

The call for business leaders to become models to the next generation, issued in the previous chapter, requires more than rhetoric. It requires commitment as well as action. Here, then, are a plan and guidelines for us to live out in the marketplace our commitments to be ethical in all our dealings.

PURPOSE TO BE ETHICAL

To make this commitment, you must purpose to be ethical, to establish a personal standard of ethics for which you will give your very economic security to meet. No amount of money will move you from your determination. No opportunity for power will pull you down from your ethical idealism. No threat will deter you from your decision. No influence, whether from friend or mentor, will affect your aim. Your commitment, even if painfully costly, will be kept. It is this that marks you as going beyond the bottom line. Few people may ever hear of you; you may never rise to the top of your company or see your business become a model for all of America to emulate; you may labor unnoticed in an unknown small town lost on the landscape of a midwestern plain. But you will become a force of energy for good, even a redemptive force that calls others away from the easy but horribly painful and destructive life to the life of sacrifice and growth and maturity that is worth living and worth passing on to the next generation. What more could you want than to be a change-maker? You can be a people-builder, a spark of light brightening the dark horizon and drawing other lights to it until it shines with a convicting power, calling forth a commitment that would never be without it. You must purpose to be ethical.

As you purpose to be ethical, here are three guidelines you should follow.

GUIDELINE #1: OBEY GOD AT ALL COSTS

Determine, before you face the pressure to mislead or lie or cheat or cut the quality or be unfaithful to your mate or pursue your career at the expense of your children, that you will obey God no matter how great the demand. Learn from both ancient and modern man.

Consider the ancient Abraham who learned a bitter lesson because he gained prosperity through a lie but lost his good name and threatened his wife's well-being. Learn from Joseph who resisted sexual temptation because he was governed by a sense of equity, of right and wrong. Think of Daniel who determined in his heart to obey God no matter what. Unfortunately, so-called secular men and women often overlook one of the most important points in the Bible, and that is how many of God's heroes served in the secular setting and not in the professional ministry. People such as Abraham, Isaac, Jacob, Joseph, Moses, David, Solomon, and Nehemiah were agriculturalists, political and military leaders, and government officials. Even the apostles Peter, James, and John were fishermen and not professionally trained for ministry. Paul, a seminary graduate and perhaps the greatest apostle of all, supported himself and others on his ministry teams through his own tentmaking business. Knowing this reality gives the Bible a new freshness for those involved in the secular arena.

Many modern men and women have made this same commitment. Don Siebert, retired Chairman of the Board for J. C. Penney, took strong ethical positions throughout his career because of his commitment to Christ. From his earliest days in the company when he managed a department in a small-town store right up to his last days when he managed the entire company and led it through a singularly successful modernization, Chairman Siebert never deviated from his commitment to truth, integrity, and concern for employee, customer, and excellence. Even when it meant the painful decision of firing someone who failed to be ethical, he did not back down. His ethics governed his career, and although, at times, it wasn't convenient or what his boss or fellow-employees or subordinates wanted, he stood strong. The ongoing success of Penney's today certainly stems from the model of J. C. Penney himself, a model Don Siebert enhanced and honored. Just as he stood, so can you, if you will trust the Lord as he did.

Peter Stannard of Perth, Western Australia, has been recognized nationally as one of the outstanding home builders in all of that nation. Once he made his decision to trust Christ as an adult, he determined that he would run his business on the basis of the reality that honesty is the best policy. He will never deviate from that policy, no matter what it costs him, even if it means losing a profitable employee over a breech of integrity. To Peter, and his wife, Judy, who does all the interior design work in their developments, nothing is worth more than their reputation for honesty, certainly not money. The Stannards call their ethical policy the Peter Stannard Commitment and divide it into four categories: philosophy, products, plan, and purpose.

They state their philosophy to be "to honorably achieve a fair return upon investment compatible with firm, trustworthy principles, absolute integrity, and complete fairness to all people with whom we come in contact." In relation to their products, they commit to seek better methods to provide the most current services so they can give each of their customers the best value possible. This includes excellence in material selection, technology, and product innovation. They plan to grow and become better, not just bigger. In their purpose they committed to direct their employees in such a way as to mobilize the energies and resources of their business to wholeheartedly serve the needs of all their customers. Here is a customer-centered commitment to business which aims to make an honorable and fair return while putting out a quality product. All of this grows out of Peter and Judy Stannard's determination to obey God in all they do, a determination which has resulted in national recognition for their company.

Interstate Batteries, under the leadership of Norm and Tommy Miller and their team of vice presidents and directors, has developed a mission statement that shows how a company can determine to obey God. Not everyone in such a large and diverse organization (with more than three hundred distributors in Canada and the United States) holds the same spiritual commitment and values, but the leadership has seized the initiative to take its stance and make it the heart and essence of Interstate's mission. (See Appendix for Interstate's mission statement. It's an excellent starting point for company owners seeking an ethical standard for themselves and their employees to serve each other, their investors, and their customers.)

Once you have determined to obey God at all costs, you must act to implement the second guideline for establishing and accomplishing your ethical purpose.

GUIDELINE #2: TRUST GOD AT ALL TIMES

No matter what the circumstance, no matter what the cost, no matter what the stress or the tension you may bear or the stance you must take or the loss you may face or the criticism you may hear, you must obey God by trusting Him at all times. Trusting God always means taking a risk when evaluated by human perspective. God doesn't place the same value on financial security or personal achievement or powerful influence as we do. He is far more concerned with spiritual growth and character than He is with the measurements we use to keep score of our lives.

We understand life in terms of how much time we have to live, how utterly final death is, and how limited the resources of money, glory, and power are. God sees things quite differently. To God, life is eternal, death is not final, and all resources are infinite. Unless we learn to see reality as He sees it, we'll always struggle to take risks with Him, yet we'll never be able to be totally ethical unless we are independent of time, death, and resource dependency and all the control these things bring. Only those who are truly independent by being dependent on God can maintain the kind of ethical stance He wants.

Trusting God at all times means relinquishing all control in every situation to Him despite the outcome. It means trusting all results to Him no matter what that may mean. It does not mean doing stupid things like failing to plan ahead, failing to provide for financial backups in case a major source of funding fails, failing to be funded adequately either in a start-up or in new product development, failing to maintain healthy reserves, or failing to do any of the myriad of actions prudent business sense demands. The risk comes when you have done all of this and success boils down to an issue of right and wrong, sometimes clearcut and undeniable and other times uncertain and confusing. In either case, whether the pathway is obvious to all or whether you find yourself in an ethical thicket, once you have determined what He wants you to do through His Word, His Spirit in prayer, and His people in wisdom and advice, as well as through people who do not know Him but who are committed to integrity, you must take your position and hold it, no matter what it costs. This is where the risk enters in. Most often ethics pay off in business because integrity and truth generate trust, but this is not guaranteed by any means, as much of history teaches us. God promises to meet our needs, but His definition of need and our definition of need may not always agree. Better to risk it with Him than to strike out on your own. Even if you gain everything you ever hoped you could, you will lose all if God does not support your decision. As Michael Josephson observed, "If ethics means anything, it means that one is willing to lose rather than lie or cheat. One who is unwilling to lose will do whatever it takes to win."[1]

From obeying God at all costs and trusting Him at all times, we turn to our third guideline.

GUIDELINE #3: PREPARE TO TRUST AND OBEY GOD IN ALL SITUATIONS

Don't just sit and wait for ethical issues to come knocking on your door. For one thing, they don't knock on your door; they come crashing through it. Ethical issues don't wait for us to prepare for them once they land on our desks. By the time they get to us, it's too late to get ready. Ethical issues come all wrapped up in pressure and stress and hurry and anger and accusation and confusion. They are more like a labeled letter bomb designed to go off in the next hour than they are a long anticipated issue. Sometimes they do sneak up on us, starting out innocently as one sentence in a letter or a suggestion made with a smile that takes on an increasingly complex and confusing and even insidious form later on. Then, if we have not paid attention to the signals, we suddenly find ourselves enmeshed in a struggle for which we are utterly unprepared, a lawsuit challenging our integrity, accusations that falsely attack our character, or some other equally devastating confrontation. Unless we work to anticipate ethical issues and prepare for them by thinking through the principles that will guide us in our decisions, we'll fail without even understanding why. Even if we do prepare and live with total integrity, there is no guarantee we won't be attacked anyway, as Daniel experienced when he was manipulated into a lose/lose situation because of the jealousy of those around him. At least he had the certainty he was innocent and could count on God to stand by him. If you have prepared yourself by developing your own personal ethical standard and strive to live by it at all times, no matter what risk God takes you through, you can have the same assurance in times of unjust attack.

My friend Floyd Wilkerson, recently retired Vice President of Administration for Eaton Corporation, uses an excellent picture to describe how he prepared himself to face times of potential ethical stress. Often in his career, he traveled to New York to do business. When there, he had to be on the streets after dark, a situation with a certain level of risk. Obviously,

Floyd stayed out of very dangerous neighborhoods, but no one can ever avoid all possible risk, so he thought through a strategy which would give him maximum protection. He always stayed on well-lighted streets; he always walked closer to the street than to buildings from which someone could step out and attack him; he always kept an eye on who was behind him as well as who was ahead of him just in case anyone was attempting to harm him; and he always had in mind some means of escape if the worst happened. At no time did he ever have to take evasive action, but he was prepared in case he did.

In the same way, Floyd prepared for ethical issues. He, along with Eaton Corporation, had a standard of truth and integrity which was absolutely inflexible: under no circumstances would he ever tell a lie. Instead, he looked ahead and anticipated the issues which he would face. Then he devised a plan by which he would tell those who reported to him all that he could about the situation. If he were asked a question he could not answer, he would either say he didn't know and would get back to them, if that were the case, or he would say, "I'm sorry, but I can't answer that." If pressed, he would reaffirm his answer, explain to the degree he could, and move on to the next issue. Sometimes he had to schedule private conversations to make certain the person asking the question understood why he couldn't respond and show that he was not attempting to avoid the issue. But he would not lie, and he worked to anticipate ethical situations so he was as well prepared for them as he was for muggers in New York City.

One of the things that helped Floyd maintain his integrity at Eaton Corporation was the firm stance taken by Del DeWindt, chairman of the board, who had seen what happened at General Electric in the early sixties when scandal sent several executives to jail for a eriod of time. He determined nothing like that would ever happen in any company where he could prevent it. DeWindt's successors, Chairmen Jim Stover and Bill Butler, have taken similar stances at Eaton. There is nothing like a leader who serves as a heat shield on behalf of those who are under him, protecting them when they do what's right, no matter what the short-term costs may be. If you have such a position, use it effectively to release those committed to the right to take the risks they must, and to remove those who won't stand for the right no matter what risk that action may bring.

IF YOU'RE LEGAL, YOU'RE RIGHT?

If you're legal, you're right, right? If everyone knows that all players are lying, no one is really lying, right? Business is a game, a game with its own rules, like poker, and as long as you play by poker rules you're right, right? These are key assertions made at times in the business world today.

We have looked at these assertions in the last two chapters and realized that if the bottom line is your focus, they may stand up in the short run. But if you go beyond the bottom line to the place where faith and business meet, these assertions fail immediately.

All these claims assume a perspective of life that is human: time-bound, death-determined, and resource-limited. We make our most profound decisions controlled by the humanly undeniable reality that there are only two things: now and no more. At their rawest, human values will aim for us to get as much as we can as soon as we can so we can enjoy it as long as we can because now is all we're going to get. Very often, compassionate human beings do seek to help others in their human condition. But our day tells us that helping others in their human condition, no matter how tragic, is not enough for a significant number of us. However, as we said, this is not how God sees life, nor is it how life truly is. For God, life is eternal, death is a doorway, and resources are infinite. As a result, He has no limits, whether it be in relation to time, life, or possessions. His values transcend time, life, and things, and He expects us to establish our values in light of His view of life.

Our ethics cannot be founded on the transient rules of a game but must be founded on the transcendent absolutes of God. This is why we must commit to God's guidelines for ethics. To be ethical, we must consider the eternal. Not only must we make every effort to establish our own ethical standards based on God's eternal absolutes; we must also make every effort through our example (always appropriate) and authority (where appropriate) to influence others to follow our lead. This must be our commitment and our cause, and when it is, it will give our lives the meaning that we seek. We then go beyond the bottom line as those willing to take any risk and pay any price to stand for what is right with integrity and love.

CHAPTER ELEVEN

ALL OR NOTHING

Doing business the way Jesus wants it done means all or nothing. Either you give Him all, or you get nothing. This is reality. Either you trust Him for all by giving up total control of your life, your career, your possessions, and your position, or you end up with nothing. No matter how much you have, how great your power, how high your influence, you will lose all unless you gained it the way Jesus wants. So now I ask, how badly do you want to go beyond the bottom line to the place where faith and business meet?

GIVE ALL YOU'VE GOT

FINANCIAL STABILITY

Suppose Jesus came to you personally and physically and challenged you in the area of financial stability in your life.

Suppose He said to you, "I want you to trust Me exclusively as your source of financial stability. I want you to give Me all you possess and every resource you have for making money for as long as you live. I want you to sign over your house, your cars, your savings account, your IRA, all other sources of retirement income, your entire portfolio, everything. I want your lake house, your time share at Aspen, any and every means you have for guaranteeing financial security. I want you to sign it over to Me so I am the Owner of record. It's not that I plan to take it away from you. You can use it, but I want to have the freedom to do whatever I please with it for My purposes.

"So here's what I want you to do. Take out a piece of paper, list all your assets, total them up, and sign the following agreement":

> I, the undersigned, hereby release now and as long as I live to Jesus Christ, God's Son and Lord of the universe, all claim on anything legally listed as belonging to me, as well as all abilities I have to earn and own. From this point on and forevermore I agree and commit myself to be the steward of all of these things and affirm that Jesus is the true Owner. Further, I acknowledge that He, as Owner, can and will hold me account-able for the way I manage His possessions and that He can do whatever He pleases with what is His. I also understand that I am totally dependent on Him for all financial security and I choose to trust Him to meet all of my life's needs.

Are you willing to do this? You need to answer *yes* to this question because this is what it means to go beyond the bottom line and activate your faith in the workplace.

SOCIAL ACTIVITY

Or, suppose Jesus came to you personally and physically and chal-lenged you in the area of social activity. Suppose He said, "I want you to focus less on your Christian friends and more on the men and women around you in your neighborhood or on your job or on your son's soccer team or your daughter's Indian Guides group. I know your church relation-ships are important to you, but I am concerned that the people around you don't know Me, and I want you to be the one who introduces them to Me.

"So, here is what I want you to do. Get out your calendar and evalu-ate each commitment to determine which ones you can drop without breaking your word or creating problems for your church or others. Can-cel anything you ethically can. Once you've done that, look at what re-mains on your calendar and plan how you can free yourself from these responsibilities. Tell those in leadership of your intentions and involve them in determining how soon you can break loose, who should take your place, what role you must play in recruiting and training someone to take over from you, and what will be the best date for you to bow out. Make certain you move as purposefully and carefully as possible so no one can legitimately complain that you are shirking your responsibilities. Then pray and ask Me how I want to redirect your time so you can make the impact I want you to make out on the street. Appoint Me the Owner of your time by signing the following document":

> I, the undersigned, hereby release now and as long as I live to Jesus Christ, God's Son and Lord of the universe, all claim on my time. From this point on and forevermore I agree and commit myself to be the steward of all my time and agree that Jesus is the true Owner. Further, I affirm that He, as Owner, can and will hold me accountable for the way I manage His time and that He can do whatever He pleases with what is His. I also understand that I am totally dependent on Him for any amount of time that He gives me and I choose to trust Him to control my time and my life according to His purposes.

Are you willing to do this? You need to be able to answer *yes* to this question in order to go beyond the bottom line and activate your faith in the workplace.

ETHICAL PROPRIETY

Or suppose Jesus came to you personally and physically and challenged you in the area of ethical propriety. Suppose He said to you, "I want you to take an ethical stand for Me in your corporation because I'm unhappy about the way marketing, sales, and manufacturing are operating. They make promises they can't keep and they allow shoddy work to go out the door, but they act to cover it up until after the warranty is past and the customer can't do much about it. You know what's going on, and I want you to stand up and stop this, even if it means losing your job and getting black-balled in your career.

"I know I am asking a lot, and it might seem very unfair. I know it could cost you your home, make it difficult to educate your children, and lessen your retirement income. But fairness is not nearly as big an issue with Me as righteousness and justice, and I want you to take a stand for Me. I will take care of you, but you will have to trust Me for your future. Many of your Christian friends will question your judgment and wonder what really happened if you get fired. I know all of this, but I want you to do it anyway. If you search My Word and depend on Me, I will give you the insight you need to be as wise as possible, but I make no guarantees that you will be able to keep your job. You will have to trust Me and take this risk.

"So here's what I want you to do. Add the following to the two statements you have already committed to":

> I, the undersigned, hereby commit myself to be ethical in all I do and release now and as long as I live to Jesus Christ, God's Son and Lord of the universe, all claim on my career and my future. From this point on and forevermore I agree and commit myself to be the steward of my career and my future, but I declare that Jesus is my true and only Career Planner and that I will live only according to His ethical standards on my job. Further, I affirm that He, as my Career Planner, can and will hold me accountable for the way I manage the gifts and talents He has given me and that He can do whatever He pleases with what is His. I also understand that I am totally dependent on Him for any amount of success He gives me and I choose to trust Him to manage my business future in any way He pleases.

Are you willing to do this? You need to be able to answer *yes* to this question in order to go beyond the bottom line and activate your faith in the workplace.

MORAL PURITY

Or suppose Jesus came to you physically and personally and challenged you in the area of moral purity. He calls on you to take a stand: "I want your stance to begin with your own model, a model of purity that gives you powerful influence because you are consistent in word and deed. This means you must make a commitment of celibacy as a single person. If you are married, you must commit yourself to faithfulness to your mate, you must teach your children principles of purity, and you must act to bring others together who have made the same commitment in support and encouragement of the family.

"You must go further; you must also have a message," Jesus continues. "You must be willing to speak up in your company on behalf of My moral standards. This will involve things like policies governing sex in the office, including sexual harassment, funding for family support systems in your corporation, policies concerning the kind of advertising you do, as well as the kind of organizations and causes to which you give money. I want you to represent me well and attractively because My purpose is to show others through My presence in you how magnetic moral purity is. People will judge you, misunderstand you, make fun of you, reject you, and work to get rid of you. Many of My servants before you have had to pay such prices for taking a stance for Me. I will be faithful to you, however, and meet your needs.

"So here's what I want you to do. Add the following to what you've already agreed to":

> Furthermore, I, the undersigned, do hereby release my body to Jesus Christ, God's Son and Lord of the universe, to be His temple and a living sacrifice for Him. In doing this I commit myself by His grace and power to live in a morally pure manner, to be faithful to my mate, to raise my children in a loving way and to teach them to be morally pure. I also commit myself to take a stance for moral purity throughout my career, using my influence in whatever positive way I can both to model morality and to speak out for sexual health and wholeness in my company as well as in society in general.

Are you willing to do this? You need to be able to answer *yes* to this question in order to go beyond the bottom line and activate your faith in the workplace.

ONE CONDITION, THREE REQUIREMENTS

Are you willing to make these commitments? Responding to questions like these and many others from the Lord Jesus Christ is exactly what it means to go beyond the bottom line to the place in our lives where faith and business meet. It means to follow Jesus no matter what He demands of us. We cannot do this unless we meet one condition and fulfill three requirements as Jesus declared them one day long ago in Mark 8:34: "If anyone wants to come after Me, he must deny himself, take up his cross, and follow Me."

THE CONDITION: YOU MUST WANT TO

Going beyond the bottom line starts with a condition, the desire to pursue the Lord of the universe more than anything else. Our commitment must be real and not phony. This is why Jesus begins with this condition, "If anyone *wants* to come after Me...." In saying "if," Jesus assumes that coming after Him is the driving desire of our lives, the great longing of our hearts. Since this is the case, He wants us to know what the requirements are. Jesus states clearly, thoroughly, and publicly what He expects because He never signs a contract or makes a deal without declaring all the conditions up front. He doesn't renegotiate. He spells everything out so there is no doubt about what we are agreeing to.

This means we must *want* to come after Him. We must *want* to focus our entire lives, all our energy, all our strength, all our assets, all our talents on Him and Him alone. Unless this is the driving desire of our lives, we will not do it, because coming after Christ is so demanding, and at times so painful, that we will never follow through unless it is the greatest longing in our spirits.

When we say we make this commitment, we must be men and women who are willing to pay any price to keep it, even to stand firm when everything crashes in all around us. We must be committed to stick it out even when criticism comes, when jokes are told about us, when pressure is put on us to be more reasonable, to give ground "only this one time," to be flexible, to realize "this is business and everyone does it in business," when our careers are threatened and our economic stability is shaken.

When we truly want to follow Jesus with passion and sacrifice, He will begin to teach us what it means to trust Him in business. He will call us to meet three requirements for whole-hearted obedience.

REQUIREMENT #1: SAY NO TO SELF

The first requirement is to say no to self. As Jesus puts it, we must deny ourselves. What is there about ourselves that we must deny? Are we some horrible, awful beings who can never say yes to ourselves? What is so bad about us that we must say no to ourselves, especially when everyone else tells us to express ourselves?

To answer this question, we must understand that there are two sides to self. One side is what people today call the dark side, that which the Bible calls the flesh; the other side is what God calls the new creation, which the Bible tells us we possess because He made us partakers of the divine nature (2 Peter 1:4). The dark side is that part of us that wants to replace God, what might be called our "God complex,"[1] our independent side that resists God's control of our lives and resents God's authority over us. It tells us, "You don't need God or His wisdom to make it in business." Further, it takes credit for our intelligence, for our freedom to pursue an education and develop our abilities, even for the "lucky" breaks that have given us opportunities to advance, get promotions, and make a good living. Because of this we say, "I did it my way and I did it myself," claiming that we can meet our needs and be secure in life on our own.

The dark side of self is rebellious. Our rebellious self looks for security, independence, and success totally apart from dependence on God and totally without acknowledging Him in any way. So we live to amass more and more yet never feel we have enough, no matter how much we possess. All of us know of the creeping recession that has slowly choked the life out of our economy over the past several years, first in the Southwest, then in New England, then in California. Real estate, banks, S&Ls, much of the foundation of the American economy cracked and crashed, bringing down with it men and women worth millions, destroying their businesses, forcing them to sell their homes, burying them in a bottomless sinkhole of debt. Self said they could be secure on their own totally apart from God, and they indulged that side of self. How much better off they would have been if they had denied themselves and passionately pursued Jesus as Lord.

This dark side of self seeks independence from God and demands to be in control of life and all its circumstances. We don't want others telling us what to do, when to come, where to go. We spend years angling for this security, working to get in the place where we give the orders while no one tells us what to do. We don't want to give this up. *Suppose Jesus really did take control of my life,* we think. *He might disrupt my comfort, comfort I spent years putting in place.* We think we are independent, but all it takes is one unexpected shift in the economy, one siege of tight money, one sudden twist of "fate" for us to realize that control is a myth.

The side of self we must deny also seeks for success on its own terms. This is the side that says, "I want to be a millionaire by thirty-five," or the side that drives for recognition and fame and will pay any price to get it, or the side that strives to be Number 1 and won't let anyone or anything stand in its way. This side of ourselves can be very nice, even decent, warm, and considerate. It's just that it is going to get to the top on its own whether or not this is what God wants. You can hear it in the words of the CEO who says he enjoys work more than anything else, more than golf or tennis or even family, when the truth is known. He admits this when he goes on to say, "My wife doesn't like it, but ... " What he just told us is that his business success is more important than his wife's needs. For him, and others like him, success is more important than relationships. But then come drugs or AIDS or anger or alienated children, and success doesn't turn out to be what it's cracked up to be. Some may not have enough of a conscience to recognize the pain they've caused their families; some may be so totally self-focused that they don't even feel their own pain. But those who do suddenly realize that their success has a dark side that their driving, restless self never told them about.

This is the side of self we must deny, the arrogant, independent side of self that leads us into the darkness away from the Light that is God. These drives for security, independence, and success are inherent within us, planted within us by God who wants us to be secure, responsible, and successful, but all on His terms, according to His means, and through dependence on Him. Our God-given drives have been co-opted by self's dark side, so we turn away from Him and to ourselves to get what He alone can give without pain and regret. Every day we must deny these driving passions and replace them with the driving passion to pursue God. Otherwise, we will spend our lifetime living in the dark.

There are four ways we can live in the dark, and our dark side expresses itself in each of these ways.[2] First, there is *the dark side of sexual desire.* As we said in "Sex in the Office," our society sizzles with sex. Sex is everywhere: on magazine covers, billboards, newspaper pages, in novels and movies. You can't even check out at the supermarket cash register line without being bombarded by magazine trash talk and sexual appeals. To follow Jesus, however, we must say no to such desires, no matter how strong they may be. This means we must prepare ourselves day-by-day to resist the siren call of sex by a decision to be pure. We do this, first, through prayer that affirms our priority. We also do this through a strategy to keep ourselves out of the places and situations in which our purity would be challenged, as well as through personal discipline enabled by the power of the Holy Spirit.

Second, there is *the dark side of spiritual pursuits,* called idolatry. We must say no to idolatry. Unfortunately, many of us confuse what idolatry is. We think idolatry is something uneducated and superstitious people from backward and far away lands do. We think it is bowing down to some statue or putting food in front of a stone idol or following some animistic ritual on the night of the first full moon. That is idolatry in some places, but it is not common in the Western world, the so-called advanced cultures of Europe and the United States. We do not pursue an idolatry that is so obvious; we pursue subtle idolatries, all of them tending to be either material or pleasurable or both. We seem to have two idols, the idol called More and the idol called Fun.

The pursuit of More and Fun doesn't look much like religion. That's the subtlety of idolatry; the gods of materialism and pleasure don't tell us up front what sacrifices they demand, sacrifices like time, energy, health, family (all false gods take the family from us), and even life. By the time we wake up to their strategy, life and all that's precious to us often is gone, and we may have only a few years left to serve the true God. Of course, neither more nor fun are always wrong; it's when they become gods, More and Fun, that they become destructive.

One way we can tell whether or not we are idolators is to look at how we measure our significance. If we measure our significance by More or, even more devastating, by Most, or by having the Best, so our car or our zip code or our office size makes us superior to others, we are idolators. If we measure our significance by the gods of Power or Position, so we must be Number 1 to be anyone, we are idolators. If we measure our significance by Fun, by being able to travel to the latest Fun spot or pursue the hottest Fun adventure or experience the greatest Fun moment at the sacrifice of God and others in our lives, we are idolators. One of the things we must remember is that our god determines our image, so that we become like our god, and we measure ourselves by the god we worship. If our gods are More and Fun, we feel good only when we are pursuing them. This is the dark side of spiritual pursuits, and we must deny this darkness or stumble and fall because of it.

Third, we must say no to *the dark side of personal interests*. All of us have legitimate personal interests, interests such as having enough to live, pay our bills, and enjoy life. But not all the ways we approach our personal interests are proper. In the chapters on power and ambition, we saw some illegitimate approaches to personal interest, approaches such as using power to advance our cause at the expense of others or being ambitious in a self-centered way so we are out to beat others rather than to serve them.

A recent newspaper article on the business page of the *Dallas Morning News* shows the futility of the selfish pursuit of personal interests. Entitled "Where the Raiders Are Now,"[3] and subtitled, "Corporate Marauders Paid Dues for '80s," it updates the reader on the current situation of those who attended the Predator's Ball in the early '80s. The Predator's Ball was "...an annual rite celebrating high-yield, high-risk debt that Mr. [Michael] Milken and Drexel started hosting a decade ago. Now the ball's sweet waltz music has turned into a dirge." Milken served a prison term; Drexel failed and is now bankrupt; Boesky has taken his ex-wife to court in an effort to get some of her fortune since his is gone; Carl Ichan lost control of TWA, the only company he took over, despite all his efforts. These were the big names of business, even the heroes for many, men who pursued their personal interests at the expense of others, forcing them to take on burdensome debt and fight for their very lives. Now, what they have done to others has become their portion, and they show us the folly of pursuing personal interests in a selfish and threatening way.

Finally, we must say no to *the dark side of social practices*. This description of the darkness within us is only a sample list and not comprehensive. It is more of a series of clues than a total description (as Paul states when he summarizes his warning in Galatians 5:21 with the words, "and the like"), and these clues help us gain insight into other dark practices which we must deny. Drunkenness and orgies fall into a category of evil that are debilitating dependencies which so debase us that we distort our human identities and behave in a manner lower than most animals. What other addictions are so destructive? Drugs and violence are perverted practices that bring on the mass destruction of the human psyche. So also is abuse in its multiple forms: e.g., child abuse, sexual abuse, wife abuse. We must say no to any and all social practices that scar our society, destroy our dignity, deny our likeness to God, and lower us to the level of the animal.

However, we not only have the dark side within; those of us who know the Lord Jesus Christ also possess the light side, the side that is filled with the light of His love, His righteousness, and His enablement through the Holy Spirit. This is the side of self that we must express, and it is only when we deny the dark side that we can express His light. It is through His Light that we live according to our divine design, the way God made us, which enables us to become what God created us to be. God gave us talents to express in the everyday world, talents that enable us to sell or manage or negotiate or lead or do any one of a thousand things. God also gave us skills that enable us to focus these talents, to sharpen and hone them to the place where we can make a contribution in life. Further, God gave us experiences that mold us and arouse passions within us. These passions fix our energies on causes, concerns, and convictions that stir others so they are moved to follow us against great odds in the midst of overwhelming circumstances. Also, God has given us spiritual gifts that enable us to serve Him and others so we make a spiritual impact, something which many of us never knew we could do. We don't deny this side of self; rather we seek to express it in the fullest way possible.

To passionately pursue Jesus, we must turn from the dark side of self to the Light of Christ within us, to a sense of desperate dependence upon Him and His resources. This is the first requirement if we are to remain positioned beyond the bottom line and maintain faith when the flood of business stress hits. Then we are ready to pursue Jesus passionately; we are ready to take up our cross.

REQUIREMENT #2: SAY YES TO THE CROSS

Only as we realize that our arrogant independence will cost us everything we own will we flee the dark side of self to a self controlled by the Holy Spirit. Then we are ready for the second requirement to pursue Jesus passionately. We are ready to take up our cross. Anyone who has tried realizes that denying self doesn't make its drives go away. In fact, resistance to the dark side of self often increases its desires rather than decreases them. Therefore, we must have help if we are to say no to self and make it stick. Where can we find this help? From the cross.

There is immense confusion concerning the cross. Some say, "My back is killing me. This lumbago is really acting up. It's just the cross I must bear in life." I have heard others say, "My mother-in-law is coming.

She's my cross in life." How tragic. We have completely missed the point of the cross. The cross was a very different reality in Christ's life, the reality of death, and it needs to be the same for us.

From their own firsthand experience the call to the cross had a powerful and gripping impact upon Christ's listeners. They had seen men take up the cross. They had heard the tumult in the streets as a mob shouted curses and Roman soldiers cracked whips over the already raw back of a convicted and condemned criminal. They had seen such a man, stripped and beaten, staggering under the weight of the heavy beam to which he would soon be nailed. They knew that to take up the cross was to enter into a death walk, a walk that would end in public shame and agony. So His listeners knew He was calling them to their own death march, in which they were to commit themselves to walk the streets of life in radical obedience to Him, giving up all claims to anything except His demands.

An instrument of death

To understand the cross, we must understand three realities which mark it. The first is obvious: it is an instrument of death for wrongdoing. This is exactly what it was for Jesus, but not for His wrongdoing; rather, it was for ours because it was on the cross that Jesus paid the penalty for our disobedience. Here He broke the reigning power of evil over us and provided a way for us to be removed from the presence of evil at the end of life. The cross, then, and what it stands for, is the means by which we see the power of the dark side broken in our lives. When we come to the cross, we come to the Lord who carried that beam on His back and who paid the penalty and broke the unrelenting power of the dark side of our lives. When we take up the cross, we come to Jesus and admit that we need Him to be able to deny the power of evil in us, that we need to put to death the attitudes and deeds which will destroy us otherwise.

A place of identification

The second reality about the cross is that it is a place of identification. We have been identified with Christ, so His cross becomes our cross, His death becomes our death, and His resurrection becomes our resurrection. This is the reason that He could pay the penalty for our wrong actions, that His power can break the power of darkness in our lives. Everything that was true of Him on the cross in relation to the penalty, the power, and the presence of evil in our lives has become true of us because of our identification with Him (Romans 6:3).

A place of deliverance

And this leads us to the third reality of the cross, the fact that it is a place of deliverance and release. For the condemned criminal, the cross was a place of cruel death; but for the ones who respond to Christ and take up His cross, it is a place of deliverance, the only place where true inner freedom can be found. This is why we can deny ourselves, why we can say no to the dark side of sexual desire, of spiritual pursuits, of personal interests, and of social practices. For Christ, the cross did not end in death; it resulted in resurrection and glorification. This is what the cross means to us as well. It means Christ's resurrection power in our lives leading to our only hope of glory, Christ in us (Colossians 1:27). Through the cross we find everything that we seek from business success, from positions of power, from wealth and possessions. The only chance for glory that we have comes through taking up the cross as Christ took it up—to go through death into resurrection and glorification.

REQUIREMENT #3: FOLLOW JESUS

Once we deny ourselves and take up our cross, there remains one last step: follow Jesus. This means we live His way in total obedience to Him. Although no follower of Jesus will ever do this perfectly because following Him is more of a pilgrimage than a destination, we must be committed to living as He lives every moment of our lives. But what does it mean to live as Jesus lives in our modern business world? It does not mean to be a pushover, someone who doesn't care about prudent investments and proper profits. Jesus expects us to make the most we can out of what He has entrusted to us, but always by taking into account not only the bottom line but what lies beyond the bottom line. This is the place where ethical decisions are made, where moral standards are established, where personal commitments are maintained. This is the place where, through the cross, we deny the dark side of self and express the new side of self which has come because of our trust in the Lord Jesus Christ.

FOLLOWING JESUS MEANS ALL OR NOTHING

Following Jesus means we give all to Him or end up with nothing for ourselves. If we try to save our lives, i.e., if we try to live in both worlds, the dark world and the light world, we'll end up losing everything. If we strive to maintain control of our lives while still seeking the benefits of knowing Jesus, we shall lose both. This is not because Jesus is some arbitrary harsh person; this is because the flesh promises life, but it actually destroys all that it touches. Jesus calls us to identify totally with Him, to do exactly what He did by taking up the cross to overcome darkness, and He does so because this is the only way we can experience the fruit of faith in business.

LIFE'S PROFIT & LOSS STATEMENT

Jesus runs a profit and loss statement on life when He raises the question, "What does it profit a man if he gain the whole world and lose His own soul?" (Mark 8:36). It's like a man who has $50 million in assets and $350 million in liabilities. If the lenders evaluated this man only in terms of his assets, they would declare him to be fabulously wealthy. But when they look at what he owes them, they are ready to haul him into bankruptcy court and force him to declare all so they can get as much on the dollar as possible. Peter Reichmann of Olympia & York illustrates this.[4] Reichmann's O&Y had a billion dollars in assets, and lenders were more than willing to do business with him. His Canary Wharf development in London, expected to cost seven billion dollars, was one of the most highly regarded projects of the early nineties. This fabulous dream of a complex of twenty office buildings totaling thirteen million square feet designed to house 50,000 workers attracted banks from all over Canada and the United States to invest with this sure-fire creative genius.

Eventually, things began to unravel, but Reichmann wouldn't let anyone in on his financial secrets. Hubris caused him to reject all advice or even to let his lenders see his financial records. He assured bankers that everything was going to be fine. But everything wasn't fine, as the lenders found when they finally forced their way into his financial records. By then, when he needed help from the bankers, none of them responded. They were so angry at being put off for so long that all they wanted to do was force him into bankruptcy.

And so the man who had all now has nothing. The man who controlled a billion dollars has lost not only a great deal of his money, but all his credibility and most of his trust, because he tried to stay in control and deny he needed help when he was in desperate need of assistance. He is starting over again, but he has lost what really matters to him, his stature and credibility. Reichman's reputation for wizardry and invincibility, as well as his mystique for magic in the business world is gone.

Reichmann's end is tragic enough, but what if he lost not only his fortune, his reputation, and his total control; what if he were to lose his soul as well? This is exactly what happens when we trust ourselves rather than Jesus. How much is your soul worth to you? How much is your life worth to you? What is resurrection worth to you?

Think of what you lose when you choose sex over the cross: your mate's security; the trust of others in you; your children's respect and their own purity, since they may well follow your example; your business reputation; your physical well-being, perhaps even your life. Is the profit of pleasure worth this great a loss to you? Think of what we lose when we choose ambition over the cross. We lose personal integrity, our best relationships, our opportunities to advance and fulfill our dreams; our financial security; our business reputation; our peace of mind. And in both cases we run the risk of losing our very souls. This will be true whenever we choose anything over the cross.

ALL OF APPROVAL OR NOTHING BUT SHAME

When we go beyond the bottom line we reach the ultimate measure of reality: the fact that Jesus is Lord. As Lord, Jesus will evaluate what we have done with the resources He entrusted to us as He said in the parable of the talents. He told us ahead of time how He plans to carry out His evaluation. On one occasion, He told a parable about a wealthy man who had to take a long trip and who entrusted significant parts of his estate to a few select managers whom He expected to make a profit for him (Matthew 25:14–30). When the owner returned, he brought his managers together to find out how they had done. One had doubled the value of his boss's investment, and he received great commendation with even more trust. Another had made a 60 percent profit, and still another a 40 percent profit. Both received approval with increased opportunities. But there was one who feared the owner, who knew him to be a demanding man who was skillful in making a profit. His fear so controlled him that he buried his stewardship in the ground, took no risk, and did nothing to make a profit for the owner.

When the owner heard that, he was furious and rebuked this ineffective manager as useless and lazy. "At least you could have put it in the bank and made 4 percent. Anything is better than nothing." And what the fearful and ineffective manager had was taken from him and given to the one who had made the most profit for the owner.

Jesus meant this to be a warning to all of us. In the parable, He is the owner, and we are the stewards to whom some of His treasure is entrusted. The treasure is life itself and the gifts and opportunities which He has invested within us to make the profit He desires. This profit is not power or control or wealth or security or any of the things we associate with success. It is relationship with Him and the character which comes from knowing Him, resulting in impact for Him among those around us. The double underline of true profit comes when we choose Christ over all else, even when it means loss in the eyes of others. The useless steward received a stern judgment, showing that those who adamantly refuse to go beyond the bottom line may well do so because they have never committed to serve the Lord who gave them their talents and opportunities in the first place.

When Jesus comes, the evaluation He gives us will be one of two things: approval or shame.[5] He will either say well done to us or reject what we have done as useless to Him, of no value, no better than putting the treasure of our lives and our opportunities into the ground. At the least, we can put it in the bank, even for a minimal profit. Then we would get some approval anyway.

BEYOND THE BOTTOM LINE

*T*o go beyond the bottom line demands that we make a choice, all of Jesus or nothing but death and shame. The profit awaiting beyond the bottom line is the profit of character that pleases God and brings you the honor of a good reputation. It is the profit of a treasure that endures beyond time into eternity, the profit of a clear conscience, of respect from your children and the confidence of your colleagues that you can be trusted, of assurance of your customers that you deliver with integrity and quality, of your mate's security that you are faithful to the commitments you have made.

But if you do not value this profit as much as the bottom line, the profit of dollars and power and passing glory, you will lose all that stands beyond the bottom line. You will lose respect from those close to you, the confidence of your colleagues, the assurance of your customers that they matter to you, and the sense of security in your mate that you are a person of your word.

Most of all, though, you will lose the approval of Jesus Himself, His well done, His affirmation that you have trusted Him and so pleased Him in all you have accomplished.

There are two great bottom lines in life, the business bottom line of profit and loss and the ultimate bottom line—life and death. The bottom line of business matters, but to decide that it matters the most is to decide that daily living is all there is, and that there is nothing beyond the bottom line of death. This is the most costly mistake we can make, to think that only what happens today matters. When we get beyond the bottom line of death and see Jesus face-to-face, we will find the ultimate in accountability, because He decides what true profit and loss are.

And so you must decide to go beyond the bottom line to the core of your conscience and commit to forge a character that counts, a character of consistent quality that models what it means to identify with Jesus no matter what it costs.

You must go to the heart of the soul where you stand in the midst of the tension between right and wrong and choose for the right no matter how foolish or futile it seems.

You must go to the inner-sanctum of your spirit and fight for integrity, not expediency; for truth, not deception; for contentment, not greed; for purity, not pleasure.

You must go the the foundation of your life and determine that your values are priceless, your commitments unwavering, your beliefs unchangeable, and then live your convictions for all to see.

You must go to the place of trust and make your ultimate choice for God and against self. For those who choose to do this, George Bernard Shaw's eloquent words describe life's greatest dream.

> This is the true joy of life, . . . being used for a purpose recognized by yourself as a mighty one; . . . being a force of nature instead of a feverish selfish little clod of ailments and grievances complaining that the world will not devote itself to making you happy.
>
> I want to be thoroughly used up when I die, for the harder I work the more I live. I rejoice in life for its own sake. Life is no 'brief candle' to me. It is a sort of splendid torch which I have got hold of for the moment, and I want to make it burn as brightly as possible before handing it on to future generations.[6]

It is beyond the bottom line where you find the Torch that ignites your life without destroying your soul, the Torch that turns you into a brilliant light for truth instead a black hole of emptiness, the Torch that inflames you with the passion and purity and power to make a difference in society, the Torch of Christ in you, your only hope for glory. Let His light so shine forth from you that men see your good works and your ethical commitments so they glorify God who made you and uses you in His might.

NOTES

Introduction

1. Warren Bennis, *Why Leaders Can't Lead* (San Francisco: Jossey-Bass, 1989), 35.
2. James M. Kouzes and Barry Z. Posner, *The Leadership Challenge* (San Francisco: Jossey-Bass, 1987), 16–18.

Chapter 1: The Exit of Ethics

1. James Patterson and Peter Kim, *The Day America Told the Truth* (New York: Prentice Hall, 1991), 235.
2. Ibid., 8.
3. H. Norman Schwarzkopf, "The Business of Ethics," *Worldwide Challenge*, March/April 1992, 16.
4. The Joseph & Edna Josephson Institute of Ethics, *The Ethics of American Youth* (Marina del Rey, Calif.: Josephson Institute of Ethics, 1990), 3.
5. J. Paul Johnson, "A Relativistic World," *Modern Times* (New York: Harper & Row, 1985), 1–48.
6. Margaret Thatcher as summarized by Charles W. Colson, "The Problem of Ethics," *Sources* No. 2, 15, The Wilburforce Forum, a division of Prison Fellowship, Washington, D.C.
7. Colson, "The Problem of Ethics," 15.

8. Ibid., 18.

9. "Harvard School Swaps Money for Principles," *The Dallas Morning News*, 1 October 1989, 7H.

10. Ibid.

11. George Barna, *The Frog in the Kettle* (Ventura, Calif.: Regal, 1990), 24.

12. Robert N. Bellah, *Habits of the Heart* (New York: Harper & Row, 1985), 27–48.

13. Kenneth R. Andrews, ed., *Ethics in Practice* (Cambridge, Mass.: Harvard Business School, 1989), 2.

14. Judith S. Wallerstein and Sandra Blakeslee, *Second Chances* (New York: Ticknor & Fields, 1989), 54–55.

15. Ibid., 107.

16. *Time*, 8 October 1990, 42.

17. Wallerstein and Blakeslee, 15.

18. Ibid., 16.

19. Ibid., 172.

20. George Gallup and Jim Castelli, *The People's Religion* (New York: Macmillan, 1989), 252.

21. Ibid., 261.

22. Barna, *Kettle*, 129.

23. Ibid., 141. "Syncretism" means the combination of different forms of belief or practice. As used here it refers to combining Christian beliefs and practices with alien beliefs and practices, which produces a hybrid sort of distorted and false religion.

24. Ibid., 139. Barna's research found that pastors felt the most frustrated of all professional groups.

25. John Silber, *Shooting Straight*, xiv.

26. "Harvard School Swaps Money for Principles," *The Dallas Morning News*, 1 October 1989, 1H, 7H.

27. As quoted in Josephson, *The Ethics of American Youth*, 18.

Chapter 2: The Toy Chest

1. Larry Martz, "True Greed," *Newsweek*, 1 December 1986, p.48.

2. Maggie Malone, "Life on the Precipice with the Arbitrage King," *Newsweek*, 1 December 1986, 52.

3. "The Mixed Metrics of Greed," *Harvard Business Review*, November–December 1987.

4. Matthew 6:24.

5. J. Dwight Pentecost, *The Words and Works of Jesus Christ* (Grand Rapids: Zondervan, 1981), 184–85.

Chapter 3: Beyond the Bottom Line

1. Arch McDonald, *In Celebration of Texas* (Northridge, Calif.: Windsor, 1986), 404.

2. Ibid.

3. Ibid.

Chapter 4: Playing with Power

1. Percy Bysshe Shelley, "Ozymandias," Lionel Trilling, ed., *The Experience of Literature* (New York: Holt, Rinehart & Winston, 1967), 1117.
2. Brett Duval Fromson, "The Last Days of Drexel Burnham," *Fortune*, 21 May 1990, 90.
3. David McClelland, "The Two Faces of Power," *Journal of International Affairs*, 1970, 7–9.
4. John D. Grassnick "Mark," *The Bible Knowledge Commentary,* (Wheaton, Ill.: Victor, 1983), 152.
5. Matthew 20:17–19.
6. James M. Kouzes and Barry Z. Posner, *The Leadership Challenge*, (San Francisco: Jossey-Bass, 1987), 131.
7. Ibid., 163.
8. Ibid., 164.

Chapter 5: What's Your Price?

1. Doug and Jan Rice are real people, although these are not their real names. Everything I write about them in this chapter is true, but the Rices did not want their real names to be used.
2. James Patterson and Peter Kim, *The Day America Told the Truth* (New York: Prentice Hall), 65.
3. Galatians 5:22–23.
.4. Hebrews 13:1–23.
5. Hebrews 13:15.
6. John 15:2.
7. Proverbs 1:2.

Chapter 6: Sex in the Office

1. *Time Annual 1991: The Year in Review* (New York: Time Warner, 1992), 53–54.
2. John Silber, (New York: Harper Collins, 1989), 211.
3. Ibid.
4. Ibid.
5. Robert T. Gray, "How To Deal With Sexual Harassment," *Nation's Business*, December 1991, 28.
6. Alan Deutschman, "Dealing with Sexual Harassment," # 124, 4 November 1991, 145.
7. Ted Guest and Amy Saltzman, "Harassment: Men on trial," *U. S. News and World Report*, 21 October 1991, 39.
8. 1 Corinthians 7:1–5.
9. Genesis 1:27; 1 Corinthians 7:1–7.

Chapter 7: Coming in First

1. Bob Carpenter, "Daytona Speed Week 1993! Gettin' Down to Business," *Circle Track and Racing Technology,* February 1993, 88.

2. Gerald Martin, "A Game Winning Pass," *The Raleigh* (North Carolina) *News and Observer,* 15 February 1993, sports page.

3. Chris Economaki, "From the Editor's Notebook," *National Speed Sport News,* 17 February 1993.

4. Gary Long, "Jarrett's Timing Right at Daytona, *The Toronto Star,* 15 February 1993.

5. Hal Bock, "CBS Went for Some Good Ol' Emotion," *Lessburg Daily Commercial,* 16 February 1993.

6. "Ned Makes the Call," *National Speed Spot News,* 17 February 1993, 14.

7. Jack Flowers, "This Daytona For The Jarrett Family," *Speedway Scene,* 19 February 1993, 15.

8. John 8:32.

9. Galatians 5:22–23.

10. Matthew 22:34–40.

11. Matthew 5:42.

Chapter 8: Hot Dog Wrapper or Stallion?

1. Ron Chernow, *The House of Morgan* (New York, Atlantic Monthly, 1990), 506–511.

2 Gordon MacDonald, *Ordering Your Private World* (Nashville: Oliver-Nelson, 1985), 31.

3. Ibid., 29.

4. Robert E. Kaplan, *Beyond Ambition* (San Francisco: Josey-Bass Publishers, 1991), 51.

5. Ibid.

6. Ibid., 133.

7. Ibid, 51.

8. James 3:16.

9. Terence P. Paré, "The Magician's Last Trick," *Fortune,* 20 May 1991, 92.

10. For a discussion of the differences between the expansive and relational executive, read 4–5 of *Beyond Ambition* by Robert Kaplan. This is must reading for anyone concerned about how to relate to overly ambitious executives.

11. John W. Dean, *Blind Ambition* (New York, Simon & Schuster, 1976), 31.

12. Kaplan, *Beyond Ambition,* 128.

13. Ibid., 45–46.

14. Ibid., 148–49.

Chapter 9: If You're Legal, You're Right

1. As quoted in Kenneth R. Andrews, *Ethics in Practice* (Cambridge, Mass: Harvard Business School, 1989), 99. Carr's article appeared in the January–February 1968 issue of the *Harvard Business Review.*

2. Ibid.

3. Ibid., 109.

4. Ibid., 101.

5. Ibid., 105; italics added.

6. Ibid., 104.

7. Ibid.

8. Ibid., 108.

9. Leviticus 19:11.

10. See Proverbs 6:16–19; 10:9-22; 11:28; 12:22; 15:6; 16:8; 19:21; 20:17; and 28:20, 22.

11. Timothy B. Blodgett, "Showdown on 'Business Bluffing,'" in Andrews, *Ethics in Practice*, 112.

12. Based on a chart presented by Michael Josephson at the Peter F. Drucker Foundation Fall Conference, November 1992, Los Angeles, California.

13. Paul Gray, "Lies, Lies, Lies," *Time*, 5 October 1992, 32.

14. Charles Colson, "The Problem of Ethics," *Sources:* No. 2, 1–2, The Wilburforce Forum, Prison Fellowship Ministries, Washington, D.C.

15. Ibid., 2.

16. Josephson, *Ethics*, 67.

17. Josephson, *Ethics*, 66.

18. Colson, *Ethics*, 4.

19. Ibid., 15.

20. Ibid., 16.

21. Josephson, *Ethics*, 1.

22. Ibid., 2, 25, 29.

23. Ibid., 2.

24. *48 Hours*, CBS television, 3 March 1993.

25. Josephson, *Ethics,* 2.

26. Ibid.

27. Ibid, 51–52.

28. Ibid., 6.

29. Ibid., 33.

30. Ibid., 17.

Chapter 10: Guidelines for Ethics

1. Michael Josephson, *The Ethics of American Youth* (Marina del Rey, Calif.: Josephson Institute of Ethics, 1992), 24.

Chapter 11: All or Nothing

1. Richard Lovelace, *Dynamics of the Spiritual Life* (Downers Grove, Ill.: InterVarsity, 1979), 90.

2. These four ways are based on the apostle Paul's description of the desires of our sin nature. See Galatians 5:16–21.

3. "Where the Raiders Are," *Dallas Morning Neus,* 16 May 1993, HI.

4. Richard D. Hylton, "The Man Who Blew $10 Billion," *Fortune*, 17 May 1993, 93–95.

5. Matthew 25:21, 23, 29–39; Mark 8:38.

6. As quoted in Warren Bennis and Burt Nanus, *Leaders: The Strategies for Taking Charge* (New York: Harper & Row, 1985), 32.

MISSION STATEMENT OF INTERSTATE BATTERIES SYSTEM OF AMERICA

As an example of a mission statement that focuses management and employees on an ethical standard for the operation of a company, we have reproduced the mission statement of Interstate Batteries. It is a good model of a statement that focuses company owners and staff on the goals of service to each other, their investors, and their customers. (It is reprinted by permission of Interstate Batteries System of America, 12770 Merit Drive, Dallas, Texas.

MISSION

Our mission is to supply our customers worldwide with top quality, value-priced batteries and related electrical power-source products and to provide our distributors and IBSA (Interstate Batteries System of America) with businesses which are profitable, rewarding, and growth-oriented.

PHILOSOPHY

Our business philosophy is to treat others as we want to be treated. Treat all our business associates with respect, with fairness, with integrity, caring for and listening to them, professionally serving them, always being a model of working hard and striving toward excellence.

OUR CUSTOMERS (distributors, dealers and consumers) are our first priority. Therefore we are committed to:

- Treat them the way we want to be treated—honestly and with sincerity in every situation
- Listen to them
- Provide distributors with a rewarding business opportunity and aggressively serve them to enhance their success
- Provide dealers with a profitable, comprehensive replacement battery program that best serves the customer

We care about OUR EMPLOYEES—physically, emotionally, financially and spiritually. Therefore we are committed to:

- Treat employees the way we want to be treated by acting with respect, integrity and sincerity in every situation
- Listen to our employees
- Provide rewarding jobs and give each employee the opportunity to reach his or her personal and professional goals within a framework of fair compensation
- Communicate goals and expectations clearly, hold employees accountable for achieving their goals, and reward them appropriately
- Set an excellent example of commitment to company goals through hard work, honesty, loyalty, professionalism and respect in all of management's dealings with them
- Create an enjoyable working environment which is fulfilling and challenges them toward excellence
- Provide competent management whose actions are just, ethical and in adherence to biblical principles
- Provide opportunities for Christian study, growth and outreach within a reasonable business framework

We acknowledge a responsibility to THE COMMUNITIES in which we live and work. Therefore we are committed to:

- Serve as an example of salt and light to our community and beyond by delivering excellence with integrity and humility
- Be good citizens who exercise exemplary stewardship in support of good works and Christian concerns

- Support and promote responsible government
- Bear our fair share of taxes

We are committed to enhancing OUR STOCKHOLDERS' investment. Therefore we will:

- Maintain a high level of accountability to our stockholders
- Operate within a growth framework which ensures a fair return on their investment
- Act as good stewards in handling the assets of the corporation

Moody Press, a ministry of the Moody Bible Institute,
is designed for education, evangelization, and edification.
If we may assist you in knowing more about Christ
and the Christian life, please write us without obligation:
Moody Press, c/o MLM, Chicago, Illinois 60610.